CLASSROOM PROBLEMS IN THE EDUCATION OF GIFTED CHILDREN

BY

THEODORE SPAFFORD HENRY
A. B. Hedding College, 1903
A. M. University of Illinois, 1916

THESIS

Submitted in Partial Fulfillment of the Requirements for the

Degree of

DOCTOR OF PHILOSOPHY

IN EDUCATION

IN

THE GRADUATE SCHOOL

OF THE

UNIVERSITY OF ILLINOIS

1917

CLASSROOM PROBLEMS IN THE EDUCATION OF GIFTED CHILDREN

BY

THEODORE SPAFFORD HENRY

A. B. Hedding College, 1903

A. M. University of Illinois, 1916

THESIS

Submitted in Partial Fulfillment of the Requirements for the

Degree of

DOCTOR OF PHILOSOPHY

IN EDUCATION

IN

THE GRADUATE SCHOOL

OF THE

UNIVERSITY OF ILLINOIS

1917

TABLE OF CONTENTS

EDITOR'S PREFACE

If any apology is needed for bringing to the attention of members of the Society the work of one of my former associates, it will be found in the significance of the work itself. To anyone who notes the evolution of educational thought and practice, it must be evident that one of the most clearly evident tendencies of the present day is the "psychologizing" of instruction—the fitting of educational agencies to the needs of the individual pupil. For several years we have recognized the needs of pupils of subnormal mentality. We are now perceiving more clearly the even more crying needs of pupils of supernormal mentality. This *Yearbook* ought to render these needs more evident and at the same time point out how in some measure they may be met.

G. M. W.

CLASSROOM PROBLEMS IN THE EDUCATION OF GIFTED CHILDREN*

INTRODUCTION

One of the most significant of modern tendencies in educational administration is revealed in the widespread attempts which are being made to adjust the subject matter and methods of the school to the varying needs and capabilities of the children whom it is the purpose of the school to serve. Instead of holding to a rigid scheme of gradation, adjusted to the theoretical "average child," to which all children must be made to conform, those who are in charge of public-school systems are coming to see the advisability of making a more flexible arrangement and a more careful adjustment to the varying aptitudes and capacities of the members of the school population. In other words, there is going on something which has been termed the "psychologizing" of school organization, as well as of school instruction.

Naturally enough, in the movement better to adjust the school to the individual child, as well as to the needs of society, deficient, defective, and subnormal children first came in for attention. They appealed to our sympathy and philanthropy. They were considered a detriment to the work of the normal pupils. It was evident that at best they would be more or less of a burden upon society after their schooldays, as well as in their childhood, and that, therefore, whatever the school might do toward better fitting them to make their own way would be a distinct service to society, as well

* This investigation was suggested and directed by Dr. Guy M. Whipple, at that time Professor of Education in the University of Illinois, now of the University of Michigan. Material assistance in its pursuit was received from Miss Genevieve Coy, at present connected with the Department of Psychology, Ohio State University, and Dr. H. T. Manuel, Professor of Psychology in the Gunnison, Colorado, State Normal School. Acknowledgements are also due the large number of public school officials and teachers who responded to requests for information.

as a benevolence to the afflicted. As a result of the interest aroused in the education of such children, there has developed a distinctive pedagogy of subnormal children, which has assumed quite respectable proportions.

While no one could object to what has been done to make life less burdensome to those who have entered into it under handicaps so heavy, it cannot be denied that if differentiation of instruction is to be confined to those at the lower end of the scale of mental ability, such differentiation is at best one-sided. A division of classes which is made merely by separating from the average those who fall below it is a step in the right direction, but a step that needs another to complement it. In order to bring about a proper balance, provision should also be made for those more fortunate individuals, who, by reason of better and larger gifts, stand at the upper end of the scale. This one-sidedness has only lately begun to receive the attention of educators. Interest in special provision for children of superior mental powers was first exhibited by practical schoolmen. Harris in Saint Louis, Van Sickle in Baltimore, Kendall in Indianapolis, as well as others, became interested in the subject, and not only put into operation within their own school systems, schemes for adapting the school program to the peculiar and distinctive needs of the bright child, but did much in their publications and addresses to arouse a similar interest in other quarters. Petzoldt,[1] in Germany, has carried on an active campaign for the establishment of special schools for gifted children, and has not been daunted by the rather fierce attacks of his critics; while Sickinger, at Mannheim, included in his well-known system provision for such pupils as were fitted to do extra work.

The efforts of these practical school administrators have been given impetus by those psychologists who have been contributing to the psychology of individual differences. Stern has not only given us his important work on individual psychology,[2] but has made a definite plea for special classes for such pupils as are endowed with

[1] Petzoldt, J. Sonderschulen für hervorragend Befähigte. *Neue Jahrbücher für die Pädagogik*, 14: 1905, 425–456. Also Die Einwände gegen Sonderschulen. *Neue Jahrbücher für Pädagogik*, 28:1911, 1–24.

[2] Stern, W. *Die differentielle Psychologie.*

superior general intelligence.[3] In America, Goddard, Terman,[4] and Whipple[5] have done much to further the interest in special educational facilities for bright children, especially the last-named, to whom we owe the term "gifted" as the standard designation of children of supernormal ability. All these efforts have had their effect, and it is safe to say that at the present time there is a wide and growing interest in the education of the supernormal child and the best means by which it may be brought about. During the past ten years these topics have received increased attention in the meetings of the National Education Association, the reports of the United States Commissioner of Education, the bulletins of the Bureau of Education, and in the various school journals. Many cities and towns are already making special provision for gifted pupils, either by schemes of flexible grading, or by special rooms or classes for them, and others are definitely planning to make such provision as soon as it may be possible or feasible.

The arguments in favor of special educational provision for bright children are both social and individualistic. From the former standpoint, society cannot afford the loss entailed upon it by the incomplete development of its most able and competent members. On the individualistic side, every child, whether subnormal, normal, or supernormal, has a right to that kind of education which is best suited to his powers and his needs. There is a moral question involved, also. It is just as important for the bright child to acquire correct habits of work as it is for the dull or average child to do so, whereas in the ordinary class the brightest children are likely to have from a fourth to a half of their time in which to loaf, and never or rarely have the opportunity of knowing what it means to work up to the limit of their powers. The consequent habits of indolence, carelessness, and inattention, which are so likely to be formed under such conditions, might be avoided by the provision, for such children, of special courses of such a nature as to fit their peculiar characteristics.

[3] Stern, W. The supernormal child. *Journal of Educational Psychology*, 2: March, April, 1911, 143–148, 181–190.

[4] Terman, L. M. *The Intelligence of School Children*. Boston, 1919. Especially Chs. 10 and 11.

[5] Whipple, G. M., Supernormal children, in Monroe's *Cyclopedia of Education*. Also *Classes for Gifted Children*, Bloomington, Ill., 1918.

Although the arguments for special provision for gifted children are coming more and more to be recognized as valid, and notwithstanding the general and growing interest in the education of the superior child, we have in the pedagogy of very bright children a field as yet practically untouched. From the Report of the United States Commissioner of Education for 1915 I quote the following paragraph:

"The public is becoming interested in the supernormal child; the press is eager for information regarding this type of child; and the school is rapidly becoming aware that it has neglected this problem. Rapid advancement classes are held for these children in certain cities, in others extra work is given them in the regular classes. But as yet few cities have had the courage to develop a program exactly fitted to their needs, nor have the psychological clinics said much regarding tests to discover the supernormal."[6]

It is within this neglected field of the pedagogy of gifted children that this study aims to make its contribution. The study is based upon the observation of the experimental room which is described at a later place in the text. This room was under the author's constant oversight, and he had the privilege of doing some teaching in it. Other information was obtained through the inspection of two different types of special rooms for bright children, which form a part of the school system of Louisville, Kentucky. An investigation has also been made of a large number of school reports of various cities, and an extensive correspondence has been carried on with city superintendents whose school systems include definite and special provision for bright children, as well as with teachers in charge of special groups or classes of such children. Other rooms of the same grade in the school in which the experimental room was located afforded a control group for the purpose of various educational and psychological tests which were given to both groups by a trained psychologist, and upon the results of which many of the conclusions of the study are based. The author found that the experience he had obtained in twelve years of teaching and supervision in public-school systems was of material assistance in his observation of the experimental room and in fact led him to generalizations that might not have been possible without this background of experience with ordinary elementary-school classes.

[6] *Report of United States Commissioner of Education*, 1915, Vol. I, p. 40.

CHAPTER I

FLEXIBLE PROMOTION SCHEMES AS RELATED TO THE SCHOOL PROGRESS OF GIFTED CHILDREN

Many efforts have been made in various localities toward the solution of the problem of making school promotion fit different intellectual grades—ungraded classes, more rapid promotion through special coaching and through systems of flexible grading, methods of dividing grades into groups according to intellectual ability and progressing at different rates, etc. The different provisions for flexible grading which have been, or are now, in vogue in different places have been so well described by others as to render unnecessary any lengthy or detailed discussion of them at this time.[1] At the risk of unnecessary repetition, however, it has been thought best to give a brief treatment of them, both because they are related to the general question of the school progress of gifted children, and also because, historically speaking, out of these the special room or class for gifted pupils has evolved.

To Dr. W. T. Harris, Superintendent of the Saint Louis schools from 1867 to 1880, and United States Commissioner of Education from 1889 to 1906, is due the credit for the first comprehensive plan to introduce flexibility into the classification of the graded school. The features and merits of his plan are discussed in his reports for 1868–69 and 1871–72–73. He described his scheme before the members of the National Education Association in 1872, and in 1874 he included in his report a still more detailed account of the plan.[2] It is based upon a short-interval system of promotion by which pupils, at least in the lower grades, are promoted every five

[1] Holmes, W. H., *School Organization and the Individual Child.*

McDonald, R. A. F., *Adjustment of School Organization to Various Population Groups.* Teachers College, Columbia University, Contributions to Education, No. 75.

Van Sickle, J. H., Witmer, L., and Ayres, L. P., Provision for Exceptional Children in Public Schools. *United States Bureau of Education, Bulletin 1911, No. 14.*

[2] In addition to the reports cited above, see also, by the same author, Class Intervals in the Graded Schools, *Proc. Nat. Educ. Assoc.*, 1900, pp. 323–340.

weeks, with an arrangement which makes it possible for the few best pupils in each section or class to be united with the class or section next above them. This plan is of special interest to us because it is primarily a plan for hurrying along bright pupils for the purpose of keeping the upper grades from being depleted by withdrawals, and one of the features which Dr. Harris urged in its favor was that it tends to hold bright pupils up to the work of which they are capable and keeps them from acquiring habits of carelessness and listlessness.

At the meeting of the National Education Association in 1898, considerable time was devoted to a discussion of the topics of grading and promotion, with reference to the needs of the individual pupil.[3] Just at this time, there were a few schoolmen who were very enthusiastic over the matter, and were doing all in their power to get others to share their enthusiasm. It was not until about the year 1900, however, that they were able to make much impression upon the general indifference that had prevailed. It may be said, then, that the year 1900 marked a very radical change in the general attitude toward flexibility within the school organization, so that one of the distinctive characteristics of the period since then has been an enthusiastic endeavor to provide for individual differences among pupils, even to the extent of organizing special classes or special schools for students whose interests are of different kinds and who are of different degrees of ability.

This change of attitude was due largely to the activities of two men (besides Dr. Harris)—Superintendent Preston W. Search, of Pueblo, Colorado, and Superintendent W. J. Shearer, of Elizabeth, New Jersey. The latter, about 1886, had devised what is known as the "Elizabeth Plan," and in 1898 published a book devoted to its merits.[4] This plan does not differ radically from the Saint Louis plan; its dominant feature consists in grouping together in separate rooms those pupils who are of about equal ability and attainments. Each of the eight grades, accordingly, is divided into three or four sections. Each section is allowed to do as much work as it can and to advance as rapidly as it is able, while as soon as a pupil shows that he is capable of handling the work of the next section, he is

[3] *Proc. Nat. Educ. Assoc.*, 1898. Papers on Grading and Promotion.

[4] Shearer, W. J., *The Grading of Schools*, 1898.

promoted without any formal examination. It will be seen at once that, like the Saint Louis plan, this plan is essentially a device for accelerating the progress of the more competent pupils.

The plan devised by Superintendent Search is known as the "Pueblo Plan," and is different from the two which have just been mentioned, in that class instruction is done away with, and the individual determines his own rate of progress. In 1901 Search published his book: *An Ideal School*, in which considerable space is devoted to a discussion of the different degrees of ability to be found within the membership of an ordinary high-school class. He describes an experiment conducted with a Caesar class in the Central High School, of Pueblo, in which 24 pupils worked one and one-half hours a day for 100 days under individual instruction, without any home work, and says that the study "shows conclusively that even in a 'well-graded class' there are some pupils who can do three times as much work as others." He also refers to a similar experiment carried on at Holyoke, Massachusetts, where 24 members of a class in arithmetic were permitted to travel each at his own rate for a given period of time, and in which similar results were obtained, without any sacrifice of quality for the sake of quantity on the part of the more rapidly moving members of the class.[5] While Search argues that his plan gives rapid workers "full, free opportunity to live up to the best that is within them," the chief aim in practice seems to have been to take care of the backward pupils, rather than of those who might be able to advance more rapidly than usual.

One of the best known of the schemes for flexible grading is the "Double-Track Plan," or "Cambridge Plan," as developed in the city of that name in Massachusetts. This plan came into existence about 1891, and was a modification of the last six years of a nine-year course. Special, or "coach" teachers were employed to aid those pupils who seemed unable to do the work in the regular time, as well as to aid in the progress of those who appeared capable of doing the work in less than the allotted six years. On one 'track' the course was divided into six sections, on the other into four; each section covered a year's work. Those pupils who took this course in six years were classified in the regular grades, while those who took it in four years were classified in four grades—A, B, C, and D. Pupils

[5] Search, P. W. *An Ideal School*, pp. 28–32.

promoted to the grammar schools began the first year's work together, but after two or three months they were divided into two sections, upon the basis of their ability. The upper section, composed of the brighter pupils, completed one-fourth of the course of study in the year, while the other division completed only one-sixth. It was also possible for the pupil to change from the fast to the slow 'track,' or *vice versa,* at the middle of the course, and thus to finish the course in five years.

In the form in which it has just been described, this plan was in operation in Cambridge about 17 years. During this time 10,203 pupils graduated from the grammar schools, of whom 7 per cent completed the course in four years, 28 per cent in five years, 50 per cent in six years, and 15 per cent in seven or more years. In 1910, a modification of this plan was introduced. The basal course of the new Cambridge plan is eight years in length, and each year, except the last, is divided into three grades. The last year comprises only two grades, which makes a total of twenty-three grades for the eight years. Each of these grades covers the work of about three months, except in the eighth year, where the grade is five months in length. Supplementary to the regular course, there is a parallel course which covers the same subject matter in six years. In this course there are 17 grades, so that the work assigned to each grade is about a third more than to the corresponding grade of the regular course. If a pupil fails to carry the work of his grade, he is asked to repeat only three months' work. If he is in the shorter course and fails to keep up, he may transfer to the regular course, with a loss of not more than two months' time; or if he is in the basal course and able to do more work than is there required of him, he may be transferred to the supplementary course, with not to exceed two months' repetition of work at the transfer. So many are the opportunities for passing from one course to the other, that the rate of progress may be varied to meet any need.[6]

Before the old Cambridge plan had given way to the plan as it now exists, it was adopted, with some extensions, by two small cities of Iowa—Odebolt and Le Mars, and as thus modified it goes under the name of one or the other of these towns. The "Le Mars Plan," or "Odebolt Plan," comprises nine grades, with two courses,

[6] Cambridge, Mass., School Committee: Annual Reports, 1908, 1910.

one of six and the other of nine years. These courses are parallel and so arranged as to permit a transfer of pupils from the one to the other at several different points. The six-year course is divided into three two-year cycles, while the nine-year course is made up of three three-year cycles. The end of a cycle affords a point of transfer, so that a student may complete the course in six, seven, eight, or nine years, according to his ability, and the superior pupil is never required to 'mark time.'[7]

In 1897, Portland, Oregon, adopted a modified form of the Cambridge plan, in which the entire course of study is divided into 54 parts, making up 18 terms of five months each. Regular promotions take place at the end of each term, and are by subjects, instead of by averages of class marks. The work of a year and a half comprises a cycle, and at the beginning of each such cycle those pupils who have come to the same point in the course of study are separated into two divisions, a fast division which is to advance at the rate of four parts of the course of study each term, and a slow division which covers only three parts in the same time. Reclassifications may take place at the end of any cycle. Those pupils who remain constantly in the first division will be able to complete the course in seven years, an arrangement which, again, is advantageous for the capable pupil.[8]

About 1895, while J. H. Van Sickle was superintendent of the North Side Schools of Denver, Colorado, he put into operation in his schools a plan which was designed to provide opportunity for the brighter children of each class to develop their individuality by doing work which was more extended and more intensive than that done by the slower members. The special feature of this plan is the provision of extra work for the capable children, to be done by them during free periods, while the other children are reciting. Home work is reduced to a minimum, and every encouragement is given to the selected pupils to depend more and more upon their own initiative and to push ahead as fast as they can. The plan is not, however, primarily a device for gaining time, as the feature of saving time in the course receives far less emphasis than is placed upon the opportunity for self-development by following out some special topic

[7] Holmes, W. H., *School Organization and the Individual Child*, pp. 39–43.

[8] Holmes, W. H., *Op. cit.*, pp. 43–45.

of personal interest, after the minimum of each study for which all pupils are held responsible has been mastered.[9]

The "Santa Barbara Concentric Plan," as worked out in the schools of Santa Barbara, California, divides each grade into A, B, and C sections. Each section must master the same fundamental principles for each of the subjects, but the A pupils do more extensive work than the B pupils, and the B more than the C. Transfers may take place from section to section within the grade at any time, and just as soon as the A pupils of any grade are ready for the work of the next grade they are promoted to the C section of that grade. In this plan, too, emphasis is put upon the enrichment of the course of study for the more capable children, rather than upon their more rapid advancement in the course, although there is opportunity for the latter to take place.[10]

In Chicago, New York, and other cities there has been in use for some twenty years a plan known as the "Group System," or "Large-School Plan." Because of the large number of pupils in city schools, it is possible to have in each grade three or more classes and to group the pupils according to ability, with the bright students in one class, the slow in another, and the medium in still others. The group system has been worked out in two ways, which are designated as (1) the "Constant-Group System," and (2) the "Shifting-Group System." In the operation of the constant-group method, the membership of the class remains the same for a definite period, and promotions are made only at regular and stated intervals. Divisions must be provided in nearly all subjects of the course, and students in the most advanced sections may pass to a higher grade in those subjects in which they are prepared to do the advanced work, without having to be equally well prepared in the other subjects. In the shifting-group method, there may be as many groups in as many subjects as the teacher thinks best, and promotions may take place at any time. The aim in the shifting group is to encourage the bright pupils to do thorough and careful work while the slow pupils are being brought up to the grade standard. The primary aim of the

[9] Van Sickle, J. H., Witmer, L., and Ayres, L. P. Provision for Exceptional Children in Public Schools. *U. S. Bureau of Education Bulletin*, 1911, No. 14, p. 38.

[10] Burk, Caroline F., Promotion of bright and slow children. *Educational Review*, 19: March, 1900, 296–302.

constant-group method, on the other hand, is to give to the bright pupil opportunity to advance as rapidly as possible.[11]

During the superintendency of Dr. F. E. Spaulding at Newton, Massachusetts (1904–14), a plan was developed which, with some modifications, has become very popular. In this "Newton Plan" the elementary program of studies is arranged in the customary eight grades, and each grade offers, on the average, an amount of work sufficient for one year. The chief purpose of the grade lines, however, is to locate teachers and pupils as to the work they are doing at any particular time; the lines form no barrier to the advancement of the pupils. The distinctive feature of this scheme is the employment of unassigned teachers, who have no regular class and whose work is entirely supplementary to that of the regular class teachers. The unassigned teacher is in charge of a special room, to which come individual pupils or groups of pupils for such special assistance as they may need. Usually the pupils who seek this help are those who have been retarded and are trying to get up to grade, but sometimes they are bright pupils who are endeavoring to gain a grade in their school progress. The system of gradation is so flexible that whenever the work of the grade is completed in any subject by a single pupil, a class, or a group, the work of the next grade is taken up in that subject, without regard to the time of the school year.[12]

A unique double promotion system, which has been called the "Double Tillage Plan" was in operation in Woburn, Massachusetts, from 1894 to 1903. In this plan the year's work for each grade was covered in the first half-year, and then gone over again in greater detail during the second half-year, an arrangement which made it possible for bright pupils to be promoted at the middle of the year, thereby doing two years' work in one. This plan was in operation during nine years, and during that time 1,252 pupils received mid-year promotions, of whom 938 obtained a second promotion at the end of the year. In the later years of the plan, the subject matter of the curriculum was increased to an extent which made it very

[11] Holmes, W. H., *School Organization and the Individual Child*, pp. 51–54.
Van Sickle, J. H., Witmer, L., and Ayres, L. P. Provision for Exceptional Children in Public Schools, *United States Bureau of Education, Bulletin* 1911, No. 14, p. 39.

[12] Newton, Massachusetts, School Committee. Annual Report, 1913. Holmes, W. H., *School Organization and the Individual Child*, pp. 63–68.

difficult to do a year's work in the half-year, and consequently greatly decreased the number of extra promotions. As a result of these conditions, the plan was abandoned, except in the first and second grades.[13]

Plans for flexible grading have become quite popular, and a great number of the cities of the country, small as well as large, have adopted some one of these plans or some modification of it. Many school systems have made combinations by picking out from two or three of the different schemes those features which seemed best suited to local needs. An example of such an adaptation to the requirements of a small system is found in a plan of grade promotion which has been worked out by Superintendent P. F. Neverman, of New Richmond, Wisconsin, and which is in operation at the present time in his schools. Superintendent Neverman bases the "New Richmond Plan" upon the conviction that the ordinary child, as well as the child of exceptional ability, can do the work of the eight grades in less than the allotted time; that the association in the same classes of average, superior, and slow pupils is hurtful to all the pupils, no matter of which type, that all children should be together during the first grade; and that all should do all the work called for in the program of studies. When children enter the first grade of the New Richmond schools, they are treated as individuals of equal ability, but later in the year they are separated into A and B sections, which are adjusted and readjusted throughout the whole year. At the end of the year, a careful list is made of all the especially apt children who have been regular in their attendance, and who are physically in good condition, and they are promoted to the A class of the second grade, while the rest of the first-grade pupils who earn promotion go to the B section. The A section will do one and one-third year's work during the second year, while the B section is doing only the regular year's work, and will thus gain one-third of a year. If at any time a child in the B section develops to such an extent that he appears able to do more work than his class is doing, he may be transferred to the A section at once. This arrangement holds through the fourth grade, at the end of which time the pupils who have

[13] McDonald, R. A. F. *Adjustment of School Organization to Various Population Groups.* Teachers College, Columbia University Contributions to Education, No. 75, p. 95. See also *Woburn, Massachusetts, School Committee. Annual Reports*, 1903, 1904.

remained in the A section have completed the fifth-grade work and are promoted to the junior high school, and the members of the B section take up the work of the fifth grade, in which there is only one section.[14]

Similar plans of grouping children according to their ability, especially in the lower grades, are found in many parts of the country. In Carthage, New York, for instance, all entrants who are unable to read, begin their school work in the first grade in much the same fashion. Gradually they are regrouped so as to form three divisions, of which the first, made up of the most capable, completes a certain amount of work in one year. The second group is allowed one and one-half years in which to do the same amount of work, and the third group does it in two years. Before the close of the first year, it may have happened that each of the three groups has been redivided into higher and lower groups.[15] Bloomington, Indiana, has the plan of grouping the bright children together in any grade, especially in the primary grades, and these bright groups are permitted to advance through the regular course of study in a shorter time than the other grades.[16] In Johnstown, Pennsylvania, for several years the upper-grade children have been congregated in one building and the lower-grade children in another, and the various sections of the same grade have been divided into fast, intermediate, and slow-moving groups. Each group covers the entire work for the year, but the bright group not only covers it more thoroughly, but more intensively than the other groups, and invariably gains time. In the school-year 1915–16 about 12 per cent of the pupils in the elementary schools gained from one-half to one year of school time; 44 per cent of those that made time in the first half-year were in the first three grades; and in the latter half, 80 per cent were in the first three grades.[17]

At Arlington, Massachusetts, the plan of grouping pupils according to their ability is extended to the high school. In the Arlington

[14] Neverman, P. F. New Richmond plan of grade promotion. *American School Board Journal*, 54: January, 1917, 38.

[15] Deffenbaugh, W. S. Current Progress in Schools of Cities of 25,000 Population or Less, *United States Commissioner of Education, Report*, 1914, Vol. I, p. 97.

[16] Letter from Superintendent W. A. Myers.

[17] Letter from Superintendent J. N. Adee.

High School, pupils of about the same ability, as determined by the teachers' observations and the pupils' grades for the previous year, are grouped together at the beginning of the year. At the end of the first two months, any cases of obvious misplacement are dealt with by means of redistribution, and whatever changes in grouping seem necessary are made every two months thereafter throughout the year. In every subject in which the plan is used there are three classifications, rated as (1) honor, (2) medium, and (3) slow. The honor groups do more work in a given subject than the medium and slow, but the latter are expected to cover at least the minimal requirements for promotion. The work done by the medium and slow groups is said to be about the same as that required of a regular class, based on the traditional methods of selection. In order to earn promotion in any group a pupil must have an average better than D (67-69). Marks below B (80-89) are seldom found in the honor groups and marks above C (70-79) are seldom found in the slow groups.[18]

The plan of promoting by separate subjects, rather than by the average mark for all subjects in the grade, sometimes works to the advantage of the bright pupils by making it easier for them to catch up with the grade above them, especially when there is added a provision for individual promotion. Superintendent A. N. Farmer, who used such a scheme in the schools of Evanston, Illinois, said of it, in a letter to the author:

"The whole plan is based on the theory that children differ in their abilities, capacities and aptitudes. It not infrequently happens that a considerable part of the class is forced to sit idly by while the teacher is struggling to make clear a point which one or more in the group has failed to grasp. It is our purpose to give to every child an opportunity to progress as rapidly as he is able to go. The great majority of youngsters will keep together. Those who are exceptional, either because they are slow or particularly able, will be limited in their progress only by their own ability to go on."

Because it so clearly indicates the object of this plan and the method of its operation, as well as to show how it offers inducements

[18] Clerk, F. E. The Arlington plan of grouping pupils according to ability in the Arlington High School, Arlington, Massachusetts. *School Review*, 25: January, 1917, 26–47.

to the bright pupil, I take the liberty of quoting a circular letter which Superintendent Farmer sent to the pupils in his schools at the time when the plan was adopted.

"To the Boys and Girls in the Evanston Public Schools of District 75:

"Have you ever felt that you could get on more rapidly in school if you had a chance? Have you ever felt discouraged when you have failed in part of your work and lost a whole year? If you have, you will be interested in a new plan for promoting pupils which has just been adopted.

"The reason for the change is that we want to give every boy and girl a chance to do his school work as quickly as he is able to do it. It is possible that you are strong enough to do three years' work in two. Perhaps you are able to go on rapidly in some subjects, while in others you need more time. Whatever your abilities are, we want to help you to make the most of them, so that you may prepare for high school as quickly as possible and without loss of time.

"Under the new plan we shall have two kinds of promotion, regular and special.

"Regular promotions will come twice a year—about February first and again in June. You will be required to do over again only the subjects in which you have failed. If, for example, you are a fifth-grade pupil and have done satisfactory work in everything except geography and spelling, you will be allowed to do sixth-grade work in all your subjects except in geography and spelling. These you will do with the fifth grade and everything possible will be done to help you to 'catch up' with the sixth grade in these subjects also. *Whether you succeed or not will depend on how hard you are willing and able to work.*

"Special promotion will be made at any time when a pupil shows he is able to do the work of a higher grade in one or more subjects. Suppose, for example, you are in a fourth grade and are strong in arithmetic. If you show that you are able to do much more than the class is doing in this subject, a chance will be given for you to work ahead and when you are ready you will be allowed to take arithmetic with the fifth grade. By this plan you may be able to work ahead and gain much time.

"I sincerely hope that you will think over this plan, talk it over with your father and mother and teacher. I shall be glad to have you write me about any plans you want to make regarding your present or future school work. Perhaps you will want to *earn a special promotion in some subject you do particularly well*. If so, please remember that we shall be glad to help you in every way we can. It pays to look ahead and plan for the future."

A plan practically identical with this is in use at Fond du Lac, Wisconsin. In the elementary schools of that city, promotion is by separate subjects, not by grades, and at any time when ability to carry the work in an advanced grade is shown. "When a pupil is noticeable because of excellent work in any subject and his scholarship in general warrants the effort, and his physical strength is considered sufficient, he is given special help in that subject, sometimes by a parent, more often by teacher or principal, until he has bridged the gap between his grade and the succeeding grade, and is then advanced in that subject. This is not done without consultation with the parent and a willingness evidenced for the effort to be made."[19]

The traditional, and probably the most common, method of dealing with the supernormal child in the school has been merely to let him skip a grade or a class. The most extensive study of this procedure and its results is one, as yet unpublished, made by Mr. B. Q. Hoskinson, at present Superintendent of schools at Pinckneyville, Illinois, while pursuing advanced work at the University of Illinois.[20] He studied a group of 84 college students and 44 school children, all of whom had been permitted to skip at least a half year of the regular school course. Of the college students, 67 had skipped an entire grade. Of the whole group 81 per cent had gifted ancestors; 83 per cent had healthy parents; 90 per cent were healthy as children; 93 per cent were regular in school attendance; 93 per cent were undoubtedly able in school work; 88 per cent had been urged by school authorities to gain time in this way; only 3 per cent had ever repeated a grade; 87 per cent believed that the skipping had been advantageous to them; and in 75 per cent of the cases the grades skipped had been below the seventh. As a class these accelerates were found to be rapid readers, quick learners, earnest, industrious, and able to concentrate. They were given to exploration of material on their own account, were kept in good condition at home, and had a good attitude toward the school instilled into them by their parents. The advantages to the individual most often named were the saving of time, and the opportunity for keeping busy and interested. Dis-

[19] Roberts, Superintendent J. E. *A Working Scheme of Promotional Efficiency.*

[20] Hoskinson, B. Q. *The School Progress of Gifted Children.* Unpublished master's essay in the library of the University of Illinois.

advantages mentioned were the disturbance of social adjustments, and, less often, difficulty in keeping up with advanced work. In concluding his study, Hoskinson recommends that in country, village, and small-town schools, the best ten per cent of pupils be allowed to skip in grades below the seventh, if health be sound, with some provision to bridge the gap, if only by a few hours of special assistance at home or at school.

The plan of permitting the brighter pupils to skip a part of the course has the advantage of being easy of operation, so far as surface indications go, at any rate; for it does not interfere with any system of grading or promotion which the particular school has adopted. It is objectionable, however, in that it offers nothing by way of constructive detail and does not partake of the nature of a positive program, rather having the appearance of a mere make-shift. Opportunity to skip a grade usually comes to a child only through a suggestion by the teacher; and unless the school system has some definite and organized way of determining who shall be entitled to skip grades, and some method of searching for all pupils who have the ability to do so, opportunity to skip a grade is likely to be the result of the mere chance of obtaining the interest of a teacher who has initiative and energy enough to follow the matter up. In some school systems, however, special promotions are featured and teachers are made to recognize it as a part of their duties to be on the watch for all possible chances to bring such promotions about. Thus, in Salt Lake City the plan of treatment of very bright children is by special promotion, although in certain instances where special promotion does not seem advisable, bright children are assigned supplementary reading or extra work in the fine and applied arts.[21] Much the same thing is done in Kansas City, Missouri, where, in addition to a flexible promotion system, making special promotions easy to adjust, exceptionally bright children are given an opportunity to do broader work than is given to the average child. This is done in the way of additional assignments, additional work in supplementary reading, and other special work of a similar nature.[22] In Kansas City, however, it was found that less than three per cent of the elementary school enrollment received special promotions, demotions,

[21] Letter from Superintendent E. A. Smith.

[22] Letter from Superintendent I. I. Cammack.

or double promotions during one-third of the school year 1914–15, and that it was two and one-half times easier for a pupil to secure a special promotion in the same room than to a higher class in another room, although the 'distance' between the two classes is no greater in the one case than in the other.[23] Obviously, then, even when the special promotion plan is definitely recognized as a means of promoting the advancement of bright pupils, grade lines put a limitation upon the child's opportunity to gain special promotion, and it may very well be that lack of interest on the part of the teacher, or some other personal factor, is largely to blame for that limitation.

One way in which the objectionable features of special promotion which involves the skipping of any part of the course may be greatly lessened, consists in shortening the promotion interval, so that the amount of subject matter to be made up is correspondingly lessened. On the other hand, it is clear that if that interval be made very short, many more special promotions are necessary in order to make a gain of a year or a half-year in the course, and consequently many more, though slighter ajdustments must be made. In the Saint Louis public schools, as they are now organized, each grade is divided into four quarters of ten weeks each, and when a class finishes a quarter, the members are promoted to the next quarter, even though they remain in the same room where they have been. In the larger elementary schools there are classes for each of the thirty-two quarters of the eight-year course. The time which each class will spend upon the work of a quarter depends largely upon the policy of the principal, who is given great liberty in this matter. Frequently a class will do thirty weeks' work in twenty, and sometimes one will be found able to do twenty weeks' work in ten. In addition to the regular class promotions, individual promotions may be made at any time in the case of pupils who are able to advance faster than the class. Such promotions are made after consultation between the principal and the teacher, and also, in case it seems advisable, conference with the parents. Sometimes pupils who are thus promoted recite with the two classes for a time, and then only with the advanced class. In other words, they skip a quarter. Out of 2,519 graduates of the elementary schools whose school records have been examined, twenty

[23] Melcher, G. Studies by the Bureau of Research and Efficiency of Kansas City, Missouri. *The Fifteenth Yearbook of this Society*, p. 131.

per cent had received double promotions, while eighteen per cent had failed. That is, the number of pupils who required three-fourths, or less, of the assigned time to do the work of the grades was slightly larger than the number of those who required more than the assigned time.[24]

In Parkersburg, West Virginia, whenever children are found who are capable of doing the work of the next higher grade, they are allowed to go on to that grade. In this particular system, which is no doubt typical of a great many, promotions are semi-annual, and the special promotion, therefore, involves a jump covering a half-year's work.[25] In Muskogee, Oklahoma, bright children are enrolled and recite in the regular classrooms, though on recommendation of the teacher and principal they may be permitted to skip grades. There are in the schools of that city quite a number of children who have been thus accelerated, and they are doing very well the work of classes advanced for their chronological age. In order to make up for the deficiencies which may occur because of skipping grades, principals will sometimes give special instruction in their offices.[26] In Richmond, Indiana, in the first six grades the bright children, with the slow ones, are coached by the kindergarten teachers and the principals, and, under a flexible system of promotion, are placed at any time in the grade where, in the judgment of the teacher and principal, they can do the best work.[27] Carthage, New York, provides a special teacher in the lower grades whose entire time is expended in coaching backward pupils and helping the brilliant ones to jump to the next higher division,[28] and Coshocton, Ohio, has two such teachers.[29]

At the B. F. Day School in Seattle, frequently during recent years as many as ten per cent of the total enrollment have advanced one year and a half in the course in one year's time. The school has an extra teacher, known as the auxiliary teacher, who devotes about a

[24] Stevens, W. F. Relation of progress of pupils to actual attendance, elementary Schools of Saint Louis, Missouri. *Educational Administration and Supervision*, 3: January, 1917, p. 14.

[25] Letter from Superintendent F. M. Longanecker.

[26] Letter from Superintendent E. S. Monroe.

[27] Letter from Superintendent J. T. Giles.

[28] *United States Commissioner of Education*, *Report*, 1914, Vol. I, p. 97.

[29] Letter from Superintendent Charles E. Bryant.

fourth of her time to assisting pupils to make special promotions, and the rest of her time in helping other pupils to maintain their present classification. Which ones deserve special promotion is determined by the principal as one of his special problems in supervision, and in conference with the teachers interested. Many of the courses of study allow for a minimum in special cases—an arrangement which is often of advantage in this connection, for in some cases the specially promoted pupil is not held to covering all the material in the course. If some of the ability to do advanced work depends more upon the pupils' ability than upon a definite amount covered in the preceding grades, they may be allowed to skip part of such work entirely.[30]

An examination of the different plans of grading and promotion which we have discussed, including the various plans for special promotions or skipping of classes, will show that each of them makes some provision for capable children in at least one of the following three ways: (1) they do more work than ordinary pupils, but in the same time; or (2) they do a different kind or type of work, with no gain of time; or (3) they are allowed to do the same work, or work differing only slightly from it, but in less time. At first thought, it might seem as if among these different arrangements there might be found one that would fit ideally the needs of the gifted child, but, while they are better than no arrangement at all, they do not, in our judgment, afford the best kind of adaptation of school work to the child whose performance stands out as of a quality far above the average. The schemes for flexible grading, because of the desire on the part of teachers and principal to maintain something like an equality of numbers in the membership of the different classes or groups, operate in such a way as to make the selection of rapidly advancing pupils too broad, unless a considerable number of different groups is provided within each grade; while in the schemes for special promotion, or skipping grades, selection is too likely to rest on mere accident, as has already been shown. These plans are all at fault, too, in that they make only indirectly at best any contribution to that pedagogy of the supernormal, which, as Stern points out, is

[30] Letter from Principal A. S. Gist.
See also Gist, A. S. The acceleration of pupils. *School and Society*, 5: January 27, 1917, 116–118.

needed from a sociological point of view as a counterbalance to the pedagogy of the subnormal. If defective children are entitled to special educational treatment and special study for the purpose of discovering what methods of instruction are best adapted to them, why are not children who are just as far removed from the average, but in the other direction, just as much entitled to special educational opportunity and a special pedagogy? All the arguments for special rooms or classes for the subnormal can be made to apply just as effectively in defense of similar arrangements for the gifted, or supernormal. In truth, educators are beginning to realize the need of special classes or special rooms for gifted children and they have already been established in a number of American cities.

CHAPTER II

SPECIAL ROOMS FOR GIFTED PUPILS

The development of the interest among educators in special facilities for the instruction of gifted pupils may be clearly traced through successive volumes of the Proceedings of the National Education Association, the Bulletins of the United States Bureau of Education, and the Reports of the Commissioner of Education. The discussion of the Saint Louis plan of grading by Dr. W. T. Harris before the National Education Association in 1872, as well as the papers and discussions upon the general topic of grading and promotion at the 1898 meeting, to which we have already referred, incidentally included reference to the needs of abler pupils and explanations of how these needs might be met by the adoption of a more flexible system of grading. During the meeting of the National Council of the National Education Association, at Los Angeles, in July, 1907, Superintendent J. H. Van Sickle, then of Baltimore, pointed out the advantages obtained by making special arrangements for the education of pupils of more than average capability, and described the plans for doing this which were in use in Baltimore and in Worcester, Massachusetts.[1] C. H. Kendall, then Superintendent of Schools at Indianapolis, at the meeting of the Department of Superintendence at Washington, in February, 1908, discussed the advisability of modifying instruction in the case of brilliant pupils, and described the operation of two special rooms for bright children which had just been established in his school system.[2] The preliminary report of the Committee on Provision for Exceptional Children in the Public Schools, made to the National Council in June, 1908, contained a discussion of special schools for bright children and of the principles that should control the course of study in such schools.[3] In an address before the Child Study Section of the National Educa-

[1] *Proc. Nat. Educ. Assoc.*, 1907, pp. 360–361.
[2] Same, 1908, pp. 147–152.
[3] Same, pp. 350–351.

tion Association at the same meeting, Supervising Principal Charles A. A. J. Miller, of Baltimore, argued for a more sympathetic treatment of bright pupils and a more careful consideration of their needs.[4] The Journal of Proceedings for 1910 contains an article by Van Sickle on provision for gifted children in the public schools,[5] and Superintendent J. G. Collicott, of Indianapolis, read before the Department of Superintendence at Cincinnati, in February, 1915, a paper treating of the current methods of dealing with exceptionally bright children in the public schools.[6]

As to reference to gifted children in the publications of the Bureau of Education, Bulletin 1911, Number 14, of that bureau, prepared by J. H. Van Sickle, Lightner Witmer, and L. P. Ayres, and entitled *Provision for Exceptional Children in Public Schools*, contains a thorough-going discussion of the different methods of adapting the work of the school to bright children which were in use at that time, and in the Report of the Commissioner of Education for 1913,[7] and again in the report of the same official for 1915,[8] space is given to a consideration of the same general topic. One very significant feature which may be noted in connection with these publications is that the gifted child seems to have established his right to consideration along with other types of exceptional children, so that no discussion of the education of exceptional children is now complete unless some attention is given to the education of the gifted.

The bulletin published in 1911, to which reference is made above, states that at that time five cities had special classes for gifted children. Witmer,[9] in the Report of the Commissioner of Education for 1913, gives the names of twenty-seven cities making such provision, in addition to the original five. Wallin, in 1914, reports 22 cities as having classes for bright children.[10] Evidently, however, in both these lists there are included some cities whose provision for

[4] Same, pp. 958–959.

[5] Same, 1910, pp. 321 ff.

[6] Same, 1915, pp. 457–462.

[7] *United States Commissioner of Education, Report*, 1913, Vol. I, p. 445.

[8] Same, 1915, Vol. I, p. 40.

[9] Witmer, L. Progress in education of exceptional children in public schools during the year 1913, in *Report of the Commissioner of Education*, 1913, Vol. I, Chap. XX.

[10] Wallin, J. E. W. *The Mental Health of the School Child*, p. 427.

gifted children consisted merely of plans of flexible grading, permitting the unusually able pupil to make more than normally rapid progress through the grades, not of special rooms for gifted children only. Exact figures upon the number of such rooms in existence are difficult to obtain, for the reason that any question as to provision for gifted children is likely to be liberally interpreted. In a doctor's dissertation from Columbia University by R. A. F. McDonald, published in 1915, a list is given of 22 cities that reported "special schools or classes for exceptionally gifted pupils in their public school system."[11] I have checked up this list, and find that one of these cities has never had any other provision for gifted children than an occasional special promotion, another has had a room for backward children, but never one for the gifted, one has a "mixed" room for both dull and gifted(!), and two provide auxiliary teachers who, in addition to coaching backward pupils, give assistance to pupils who are trying for special promotion. In 1917 Miss Elizabeth L. Woods stated that 45 cities had classes formed of gifted children only,[12] but I am sure that these figures were too high, if by "classes" is meant groups of children which are definitely formed for the purpose of receiving a type of instruction different from that given the rest of the school. The more rapidly moving groups which form a part of many of the schemes of flexible grading do, it is true, closely approximate special classes for gifted children, but they are not so definitely established as rightly to be considered special classes, nor is the basis of selection such as to entitle them to the title "gifted," except, perhaps, in a few instances.

In the following discussion of special classes for very bright children, only those will be mentioned which are definitely known to have been established for the particular purpose of meeting the needs of children of marked ability. It is not claimed that the list given here is at all complete even for the spring of 1917 when it was made, but it is authentic, and comprehensive enough to furnish representative illustrations of the various types of such rooms or classes as have existed or are in existence at the present time.

[11] McDonald, R. A. F. *Adjustment of School Organization to Various Population Groups.* Teachers College, Columbia University, Contributions to Education, No. 75.

[12] Woods, Elizabeth L. Provision for the gifted child. ***Educational Administration and Supervision***, 3: March, 1917, 139–149.

In 1900, in one of the public schools of New York City there were organized "rapid advancement classes," which concerned themselves exclusively with bright pupils. This arrangement still obtains; that is, principals of individual schools are given permission to organize special classes for the rapid advancement of bright pupils. Many principals organize so-called "plus" classes for the purpose of enabling pupils to cover two terms in one or three terms in two. These classes are formed of exceptionally bright children, though occasionally 'hold-overs' from the term before are admitted. Accelerated classes of another type, known as "E" classes, exist, but these classes are formed to enable over-age pupils to gain a term or two, rather than to hasten the progress of bright pupils. About 1915 rapid-advancement classes were organized in three schools for the purpose of covering the seventh-, eighth-, and ninth-years' work, that is, the last two years of the elementary school and the first year of the high school, in two years. Some among these classes were formed in the Speyer School as an annex to Public School 43, Manhattan. Specially good teachers were selected, and very considerable help was given by the teachers from Teachers College.[13]

The first really definite provision for the acceleration of capable children seems to have been made, however, at Worcester, Massachusetts, where, in September, 1901, so-called "preparatory schools" were opened for the purpose of helping the able child of the upper grades. This plan, we understand, is still in operation. Pupils selected from the different schools of the city are gathered at convenient centers to receive instruction from teachers of more than ordinary ability. At first, these schools received pupils from grades seven, eight, and nine, but entrance from the seventh grade has since been discontinued. In addition to the regular work of the remaining grammar grades, work is given in English, French, German, and Latin; so that after two years of work in these preparatory schools, the pupils enter the high school with a full year's credit in English, French, German, or Latin, and without having slighted any of the grade subjects.[14]

In the fall of 1902, through the efforts of Superintendent J. H. Van Sickle, there were established in Baltimore special classes

[13] Letter from Acting Superintendent Gustave Straubenmüller.

[14] Worcester, Massachusetts, Public Schools. *Annual Reports*, 1902, 1904, 1912.

known as "preparatory centers," which were quite similar to Worcester's preparatory schools. At present (1917) there are three of these preparatory centers in the city, all organized on the departmental plan. The first step in the selection of pupils for these centers is the sending of a circular from the superintendent's office to each elementary-school principal, asking him to have his sixth-grade teachers make out a card for each student in that grade, showing attendance, studiousness, application, ability, and likelihood of success in the work of the preparatory center. These cards are turned in at the superintendent's office where they are gone over and the selection made. A printed circular is then sent out to the parent of each child in the selected group, in order that the arrangement may be fully understood by all.[15] This circular gives such a complete and lucid explanation of the formation and work of the preparatory centers that I take the following quotation from it:

> "Those children who have made a sufficiently good record in the sixth grade may either continue their schooling in the regular seventh and eighth grades, or they may complete the elementary school course in the seventh- and eighth-grade preparatory classes, as their parents prefer.
>
> "In the preparatory classes the regular studies of the grades are continued, but Latin and a modern language, German or French, are offered as additional studies of *high school* grade, together with advanced work in English. In these three extra studies *credits* are allowed which count toward the high-school diploma. The experience of the past thirteen years shows that pupils that have been successful in preparatory-school work can complete the higher course in the Baltimore City College or the girls' high schools in three years, thus saving one year.
>
> "The School Board has authorized (if numbers permit) the arrangement of the studies in the preparatory centers so that boys preparing for the Polytechnic Institute may take advanced work in mathematics instead of Latin. In this way, although there may be no shortening of the time required to secure the Polytechnic Institute diploma, the start that the boys will have secured in high-school mathematics, German, and English, will make their work in the Institute decidedly lighter during the first year and increase their chances of success as Institute students.

[15] Patterson, M. Rose. A Preparatory Center in Baltimore, William Rinehart School No. 52. *Atlantic Educational Journal*, 12: January 1917, 234–238.

"It is essential that pupils who enter these classes shall be of good ability, studious in their habits, and regular in attendance. The amount of work required does not exceed that which such pupils, if in good health, can easily accomplish by systematic and daily effort. The extra studies are a help in the regular studies. A child who is studying Latin or German or French is in a very real sense studying English too; his mastery of English is made easier, not harder, by his study of the foreign language side by side with his English. In early years, also, one can most easily master the elements of a foreign language.

"In preparatory classes a one-session day is held, from 9 a.m. to 2 p.m. High-school hours are observed on account of the distance of the preparatory centers from many of the homes. Since little study time can be had in school, pupils who enter these classes need to devote not less than two hours each day to home preparation of lessons."[16]

Two preparatory centers similar to those in Baltimore were established in Indianapolis in 1908. These were also organized upon the departmental plan and were open to pupils ready for the seventh grade. Their membership was limited to twenty-five, and a half year of high-school work was gained.[17] At present (1917) there is only one such special class in the city. This is formed from children selected from the 'A' classes of the seventh grade, and its members finish the remaining year and a half of elementary-school work in a year, at the same time doing enough work in Latin and algebra to secure half a year of high-school credit. They are consequently able to enter the high school with a saving of a year's time, one half of which has been gained from the grades, and the other half from the high school.[18]

In Cincinnati, in September, 1910, a class for superior children was organized in the Eleventh District School, with the design that each member be permitted to pursue his own course, under proper guidance, without regard to the progress of his companions, and with the expectation that it might be possible to accomplish much more than an ordinary year's work. For this class, 32 pupils were selected

[16] Superintendent C. J. Koch. *Preparatory Class Circular*, January 14, 1916.

[17] Kendall, C. N. What modifications are necessary to secure suitable recognition for pupils of varying ability, particularly the ablest? *Proc. Nat. Educ. Assoc.*, 1908, pp. 147–152.

[18] Letter from Supervising Principal Lizzie J. Stearns, School Thirty-two, Indianapolis.

on the basis of the judgment of the teachers with whom they had worked. Seventeen of them were ready for the fifth grade, nine for the fourth, and the remaining were unclassified. Of these 32 pupils, 25 succeeded in doing two years' work in one, and thus gained a whole year.[19] Although Cincinnati provided no special classes for gifted children for some years after the initial experiment, it has lately been definitely decided to institute such classes; teachers have been appointed, and the director of the psychological laboratory has been given the work of testing the children who are recommended as possible members.[20]

In the same year and month in which Cincinnati established its "superior" class, Harrisburg, Pennsylvania, made provision for exceptionally gifted children by establishing special schools exclusively for their instruction. Two such schools were maintained during the year 1910–1911, and this number was increased to three in the fall of 1911. Each of the latter contained about 30 pupils selected from those who were ready to enter the eighth grade, and these pupils covered the work of the eighth and ninth grades in one year, thus saving a year's time in the elementary-school course, which at that time was nine years in length.[21] Harrisburg, however, has since changed from nine to eight elementary grades, and because of the congestion thereby caused, the special schools were abandoned.[22]

The first "rapid-advancement class" in Boston was established January 3, 1913, at the Lewis School. Thirty of the brightest children of the fifth and sixth grades, 15 from each grade, were selected and placed under the control of one teacher, with whom they remained until they were graduated from the elementary school. The upper division of this class graduated in June, 1914, having completed the sixth, seventh, and eighth grades in one and a half years, or in half of the regular time. The lower division graduated a year earlier than it would have under ordinary circumstances. The

[19] Unrich, Flora. A year's work in a "superior" class. *Psychological Clinic*, 5: January, 1912, 245–250.

[20] Letter from Doctor Helen T. Woolley, 1917.

[21] Harrisburg Public Schools, Harrisburg, Pennsylvania, *Report*, 1912. Also Downes, F. E. Seven years with unusually gifted pupils, *Psychological Clinic*, 6: March, 1912, 13–17.

[22] Letter from Superintendent F. E. Downes.

second class of the kind was organized at the Oliver Wendell Holmes School, in March, 1913. It contained 30 pupils, 20 boys and 10 girls, selected from the ablest pupils of the seven sixth grades in the district.[23] In 1914, there were five of these classes.[24] In 1917 there were in full operation in Boston 13 rapid-advancement classes, formed for the express purpose of giving the bright, intelligent, ambitious, healthy pupils a chance to obtain three years' work in two. A class is formed as follows: The principal of a populous district canvasses with the prospective teacher of the rapid-advancement class, the pupils who have received promotion into the sixth grade. From perhaps six classes he selects 30 of the most promising children, pupils whose marks have been the best up through the grades, whose health is certified to by the school attendant physician, and who are recommended by their respective teachers for the rapid-advancement class. These pupils furnish the rapid-advancement teacher with a letter from their parents, signifying their permission and wish that the pupils should be admitted to the advanced class.[25]

In Louisville, Kentucky, an opportunity class for accelerated children formed in September, 1914, made it possible for gifted pupils to accomplish two years' work in one.[26] Louisville, in 1917, when visited by the writer, had two special classes for bright children, but they differed from one another both in organization and in purpose. One of them, located at the Sixth Street School, contained about 40 pupils in Grades 4A and 4B. These children were drawn from several schools in the district, and remained in the class but half a year. The aim of this class was to gain half a year in the elementary course, by covering the work of a whole year during the half year spent in this "accelerated class," as it was called. After having done this, the pupils were returned to their own schools and entered upon the next year's work. The room contained a few pupils who were over-age, because of entering school late, of losing time by sickness or moving, or similar reasons—in other words, pupils who, although chronologically retarded, are not to be classed as dull.

[23] *School Document No. 10, 1913, Boston Public Schools.*

[24] *School Document No. 11, 1914, Boston Public Schools.*

[25] Letter from Assistant Superintendent A. L. Rafter.

[26] Louisville, Kentucky, *Fifth Report of the Board of Education*, 1915–1916, p. 32.

The other class, known as the "opportunity class," was located at the Louisville Normal School, and contained ten boys and ten girls, most of whom were in the 4B grade, although there were one or two especially bright children from the second and third grades. A much more careful selection had been made for this class than for the other, in that all pupils who were considered as fit for enrollment in it were tested with the Stanford Revision of the Binet-Simon Scale by the Director of the Psychological Laboratory, and none with an intelligence quotient less than 120 was accepted. The primary aim in this room was not to gain time, though it turned out that progress more rapid than normal was made, but rather to furnish an abundance of cultural material and to give the pupils a greatly enriched course. In addition to the regular subjects of the fourth grade they were given instruction in German, which was taught entirely by the conversational method. The classroom was very well furnished with desks of the movable chair type, large, round, low tables and small chairs, a piano, a Victrola, and a good assortment of pictures. The class was at the start placed in charge of the teacher of methods in the normal school, assisted by one of the normal-school cadets. It was organized about February 1st, 1917.[27]

In September, 1914, the 55 most capable students in the seventh and eighth grades of the schools of Lead, South Dakota, were segregated into two special rooms as an experiment. The rate of progress was observed, and it was soon concluded that they could do three semesters of work in two semesters of time. This they all accomplished, and when in September, 1915, their work was compared with the students who had gone at the normal rate, the rapid group received a higher grade than the normal group. In 1915–16, two rooms were organized for the most capable students of the third and fourth grades, and they, too, made three semesters of work in one school year. The next year there were three capable groups; (1) a class of 15 beginners, (2) a class of 16 in Grade 2A, and (3) a class of 15 in Grade 4A. Of these three groups, the first was coached by the principal and the latter two by the regular teachers, who also had student assistants. It is the policy in Lead that whenever and

[27] Since this was written an account of the work of this class has been prepared by Miss Race, who gave the Binet examinations. See Henrietta Race. A study of a class of children of superior intelligence, *Jour. of Educ. Psych.*, 9: Feb. 1918, 91–98.

wherever such a group of capable students can be formed, they are segregated under the care of especially strong teachers, in order that they may have the opportunity of making faster progress than they otherwise would.[28]

In 1914, in the Franklin School, Framingham, Massachusetts, 36 pupils, selected for their scholarship and comprising the upper third of the sixth-grade pupils in that school, were formed into a special rapid-advancement class. The same teacher stayed with the group for two years, and at the end of that time they had completed the work of the sixth and seventh grades and more than two-thirds of the work of the eighth grade. In September, 1916, these pupils were promoted to the ninth grade and enrolled in the various rooms of that grade, where they did work of a character far above the average of the class.[29]

In the Central Intermediate School, of Jacksonville, Illinois, which is a departmental school given over to the seventh and eighth grades, each grade is sectioned according to ability, so that the upper section in each grade comprises a group of exceptionally strong pupils. No attempt is made, however, to gain time for these upper sections, although a different grade of work is done, so that the difference is one of quality rather than of quantity.[30] An exactly similar arrangement obtains at Lincoln, Illinois, and in the Central School at Champaign, Illinois, although in the latter instance the school is not upon a departmental basis. At Lincoln, it has been definitely planned to select from the sixth grade a class with the intention of doing three years' work in two.[31] In the Thornburn Departmental School, of Urbana, Illinois, which includes pupils of the seventh and eighth grades, special classes are formed from the upper sixth of the pupils in each grade, and these two classes prepare to enter the high school in a year and a half, instead of the customary two years. Up to the present time, two such accelerated classes have been received into the high school, and their high-school work has been fully up to the standard in every way.

[28] Letter from Superintendent Theodore Saam.

[29] Letter from Superintendent E. W. Fellows.

[30] Letter from Superintendent H. A. Perrin.

[31] Letter from Superintendent William Hawkes.

An interesting method of assisting the progress of bright children is reported from Rockford, Illinois. The Jackson School of that city has departmental work in the fifth to the eighth grade, inclusive. The staff includes a special teacher, who is in charge of a room to which the very bright pupils go for recitation. At the end of March, 1917, 47 pupils had been assigned to this teacher since the first of the preceding February. These pupils recited once a week in each study, such as language, geography, history, arithmetic, etc., but they had a lesson assigned daily for study in each subject. On Monday the teacher covered the ground of the five days' language study. On Tuesday the five days' work in geography is gone over, and so on. Besides this, the pupils did the daily work of the class above to which they had been promoted, thus doing a year's work in a half year.[32] It will be seen that, in effect, this scheme is a form of the special-promotion plan, modified to make definite provision for regular class recitations upon the work that has been skipped on account of promotion to the next class.

A number of cities are providing ungraded or "mixed" rooms, in which are placed such children as are "misfits," either on account of inability to keep up with the work of their grade or of ability to do more work. Wausau, Wisconsin, has two such rooms, advantageously located, each with an enrollment that, if possible, is not allowed to exceed 15 pupils. Three types of pupils are transferred to these rooms: (1) especially strong pupils who desire to make an additional year or half year in the course, (2) pupils who have been absent for any cause and need to make up the work which they have missed, and (3) pupils who are dull or slow in any study and need help to make up their deficiencies in that branch and so keep up with their grades. The instruction in these rooms is all individual, and pupils stay in them only so long as is necessary to accomplish the purpose for which they came.[33] Similar rooms are maintained in Durham, North Carolina.[34] Concord, Massachusetts, has nine "opportunity classes," as they are called there, each of which is for both bright children and those who must go more slowly than the normal. All grades are more or less represented in them, according to the demands

[32] Letter from Principal Mary C. Foote.

[33] Letter from Superintendent S. B. Foley.

[34] Letter from Superintendent Edwin D. Pusey.

and needs, and, since the pupils in them are usually somewhere between grades in their attainments, these classes might be called "half-sizes." It has been found in Concord that by this method some pupils can do two grades in one year, and many more can do three grades in two years. From the sixth to the seventh grades only a few pupils can gain more than a grade, and below the fourth few can gain two grades in one year. These children are so graded that the teacher is able to carry them along more rapidly and in the course of a year may have brought them to the point where through individual work, under the Batavia System, the teacher of the next higher grade may pull them up to her grade, so that in these ways they will have gained a grade in the course of two years.[35]

While we have not much information concerning special classes for gifted children in Europe, a few cases have been reported. In 1899, Dr. Sickinger, superintendent of the schools of Mannheim, introduced a classification of the pupils of the *Volksschule* according to their abilities, and organized a system of special classes parallel to the regular ones. These special classes, or so-called "furthering classes," were designed to meet the needs of those children who, while not to be classed as mentally defective, were unable to do the work of the regular classes. Sickinger's original scheme of classification was a three-fold one which separated the mentally defective and the slow from the normal, but made no special provision for the exceptionally capable.[36] In 1909, however, the educational authorities of Mannheim arranged for special foreign-language classes, in which instruction in French should be given to pupils of the upper grades of the *Volksschule* who had demonstrated by their industry and by the quality of their work that they were fitted for the extra study. In accordance with this plan, pupils of the fourth grade that had received good reports throughout their course might be assigned to a preliminary language course at the end of the fourth year, and at the close of this one-year preliminary course, those that had made good progress in their regular work, as well as in this special language

[35] Letter from Superintendent W. A. Hall.

[36] Maennel, B. *The Auxiliary Schools of Germany.* Translated by F. B. Dresslar as *United States Bureau of Education Bulletin* 1907, Number 3, pp. 43–47.

Rathmann, C. G. The Mannheim system of school organization. *Educational Review*, 53: January, 1917, 55–60.

work, and had been honorably mentioned in the matter of attainment, industry, and conduct, were admitted to the regular foreign-language classes, from which they might be dropped at any time if their work failed to come up to the standard. The Mannheim system of school organization was also in use in Charlottenburg, where the classification was carried a step further than at Mannheim, so that the very bright were segregated, instead of being left in the same division with the children of normal or average ability.[37]

In the Southall Street Elementary School, Manchester, England, there has been in use for some time a very effective combination of flexible grading and special classes for bright children, which deserves notice as a plan that is both practical and easy of administration, and might well be introduced into other schools. In this school, which enrolls about 800 pupils, the 30 brightest children coming up from the kindergarten at the beginning of each year are placed in a special class, known as Special II, to do Grades I and II in one year. The rest of the beginners are enrolled in three groups—good, medium, and weak, with chances for transfer upward. At the end of the year, the pupils in Special II are promoted to the regular third grade, where they have a comparatively easy time for a year. A few of them who are exceptionally able, however, go to Special IV, there to do Grades III and IV in the next year. Of the pupils who do their first year's work in the regular first grade, a few of the best receive promotion into Special III, where the work of Grades II and III is done in one year. In other words, whenever it is possible, it is arranged that supernormal pupils are promoted to a special class where they will gain a grade by doing two years' work in one. The typical group of accelerates begins its school progress in Grade Special II, is promoted to Grade III and then to Special V, where it does the work of Grades IV and V in one year. The promotion from Special V is to Grade VI, which is followed by Grade VII; and, as a result of this arrangement, the seven years' work is done in five. When there are not enough bright pupils to form a special class, they are allowed to skip a grade and go to the one beyond, receiving, if necessary, special help in making up any part of the course that has been missed. In all, four methods of promotion are used: (1) promotion at the end

[37] Holmes, W. H. *School Organization and the Individual Child*, pp. 61, 135–137.

of the school year by the formation of a special class to work through two grades in one year; (2) promotion at the end of a year by skipping a grade; (3) promotion after the term examinations; and (4) promotion at any time. Sometimes, besides this, at the end of the half year, the pupils in each of the first four grades are divided into two sections, and the pupils in the upper section go ahead as fast as possible, in order to get as much of the work of the next grade done as they can.[38]

[38] Shaer, I. Special classes for bright children in an English elementary school. *Journ. of Educ. Psych.*, 4: April, 1913, 209–222.

CHAPTER III

THE EXPERIMENTAL ROOM AT URBANA

In September, 1916, the General Education Board placed in the thanks of Professor Guy M. Whipple, then of the Department of Education of the University of Illinois, a sum of money to be expended in the study of certain problems connected with the education of gifted children. A part of this fund was devoted to the subsidizing of a special room for bright children, which, through the courtesy of the Board of Education of the city of Urbana and the cooperation of Superintendent A. P. Johnson, was established in the Leal School of that city. It was understood that the pupils of this room should follow the regular course of study, use the same textbooks, and be held to the same requirements as the other pupils in the corresponding grades. It was not the purpose of those having the experiment in charge to crowd the children in an attempt to see how much ground they could possibly cover, but to give them opportunity to work up to their natural pace, to keep them busy enough so that they might not form habits of lazy and careless work, and to adapt the instruction to the distinctive capabilities and needs of the individual pupils.

The School

The Leal school, in which the special room was located, is the largest elementary school in the city of Urbana. It enrolls some 400 pupils, in 12 rooms, limited to the first six grades. The teaching force consists of eleven room-teachers and a principal, whose time, however, is practically all spent in teaching. The district served by the school is a rather large one, and includes most of the University residence district as well as a representative portion of the residence district of the city itself. The building is not modern in type, and cannot be said to be above the average of school buildings in towns of this size.

Physical Equipment of the Room

Owing to various delays in securing the furniture for the room, it did not go into operation until October 2, 1916, three weeks after the other rooms had begun work. The physical condition of the room was not better than average. It was furnished with the ordinary non-adjustable school desks, had no more furniture or pictures than the other rooms in the building, and was no better equipped with books, maps, globes, or similar educational apparatus. Because of our desire to carry on the experiment under average conditions, things were left much as they were, with only a few exceptions. Since the room was inadequately lighted from the north and west, with the north light at the pupils' left, the Venetian blinds which were at the windows were removed completely. The walls and ceiling were repainted a light buff to replace the dingy and too absorptive tones, and the blackboards were resurfaced to remove the gloss.

The Teacher

The teacher in charge of the room was chosen by the city superintendent and was serving her first year in the system. Her preparation was above that of the average grade teacher, for she was a graduate of one of the best normal schools in the country, located in a western state, and also a graduate of the state university of the same state. Not including this year, she had had three years of experience in teaching in the middle and upper elementary grades, in addition to the practice teaching which she did in the normal school. During the month of November, 1916, her work was observed and her efficiency rated by two members of the Department of Education of the University of Illinois and a prominent superintendent of schools. In each case her teaching efficiency was rated as average, or a trifle above average. In scholarship, sincerity, and integrity of purpose she ranked high, but was lacking in resourcefulness and initiative. The chief hindrances to her work during the year, considered from the standpoint of the qualities needed in carrying on the work of such a room, were not matters of scholarship, but of personality, and her greatest deficiency in this respect was lack of that animation, enthusiasm, and initiative which would inspire children to engage their full powers in their work. In addition to the regular teacher, the special teachers of music and of drawing worked in the room at regular intervals, just as they did in the other rooms of the building. It needs to be noted quite clearly that all of the conditions of the experiment which have thus far been mentioned are *average* conditions. Supervision, course of study, physical equipment of room and of building, instruction—none of these could be said to be above average. The only really distinctive factor in our experiment, then, consisted in the superior intelligence of the children who made up the enrollment of the room.

Selection of the Pupils

The selection of the children was made by the principal of the school, in consultation with the teachers, upon the basis of the records made by the children in their school work, their health, industry, and application. Fifteen pupils were selected from all those of the school who had at the close of the last year received promotion to the fifth grade, and an equal number from those who were ready to enter the sixth grade. One or two children who were selected did not accept, because of fear of extra work or dislike of being separated from friends in other rooms, and others were chosen to fill their places. Of these others, one sixth-grade boy was transferred from another school. As organized, then, the room consisted of 30 pupils, 15 in the fifth grade and 15 in the sixth, representing practically the top fifth of the enrollment in each of these two grades in the Leal School. The children, upon being assembled for the first time, were simply told that they were to be given an opportunity to see what they could do, not that they were expected to cover any definite amount of work.

Composition of the Control Group

In addition to the 30 5th and 6th grade pupils in the special room, there were in the Leal School 57 5th grade and 62 6th grade pupils. These were enrolled in three different rooms, which served as control groups for evaluating the results of the various educational and psychological tests which were used to discover some of the differences between bright and ordinary pupils. These rooms also made possible a check upon progress and attendance. Forty-three 6th grade pupils were enrolled in one room, which will be hereafter designated as Room 6G. A 5th grade room contained 38 pupils and will be known as Room 5Y. The third room was a mixed room, containing 19 5th-grade and an equal number of 6th grade pupils. It will be called Room 5-6F.

Personal Data of the Experimental Group

The following table displays the more important personal facts concerning each pupil.

TABLE I

Sex, Age, and Parental Occupation of Pupils of Experimental Group

Grade	Number	Sex	Age* in Years	Months	Days	Occupation of Parent
V.	1	Girl	10	3	12	Editor
	2	Girl	10	2	4	Jeweler
	3	Girl	10	6	24	Faculty, U. of Ill.
	4	Boy	11	2	8	Policeman
	5	Girl	10	9	19	Physician
	6	Girl	10	8	9	Barber
	7	Girl	10	5	30	Clerk
	8	Boy	10	5	23	Clergyman
	9	Girl	11	3	24	Clerk
	10	Girl	10	0	1	Faculty, U. of Ill.
	11	Girl	10	5	25	Seamstress
	12	Boy	11	3	12	Painter
	13	Girl	10	3	7	Clerk
	14	Boy	10	5	27	Banker
	15	Boy	11	0	8	Faculty, U. of Ill.
VI.	16	Boy	10	6	10	Helper, Univ. Farm
	17	Boy	12	4	15	Plasterer
	18	Girl	11	10	11	Merchant
	19	Girl	11	4	6	Druggist
	20	Boy	11	6	4	Clerk
	21	Girl	12	5	11	Faculty, U. of Ill.
	22	Boy	11	9	23	Laundress
	23	Girl	9	9	30	Faculty, U. of Ill.
	24	Boy	11	9	16	Mechanic
	25	Girl	11	7	12	Faculty, U. of Ill.
	26	Boy	10	9	17	Conductor
	27	Girl	11	7	19	Faculty, U. of Ill.
	28	Girl	11	1	5	Mail carrier
	29	Boy	11	3	7	Carpenter
	30	Boy	12	4	9	Merchant

* All ages have been computed as at December 31, 1916.

There are five boys and ten girls in the 5th, eight boys and seven girls in the 6th grade. The median age of the 5th grade on December 31, 1916, was ten years, five months, and thirty days, or practically ten and one-half years, as against a median age on the same date, for the other 57 5th grade pupils in the building, of ten years and eight months—a difference of two months in favor of the experimental group. For the 6th grade, the median age is eleven years, seven months, and twelve days, in the experimental group, and twelve years for the 62 6th-grade pupils in other rooms—a difference of four and one-half months, or two and a half months greater than the difference in the 5th grade.

In order to determine whether the experimental room contained more than its share of the children of faculty members enrolled in these grades, a rather arbitrary grouping of the different parental occupations and professions represented was made, and the percentage figured for each group, first for the total membership of the 5th and 6th grades, before the pupils of the experimental room were separated from the rest, and again for the membership of the special room. The conditions are shown by the following table.

TABLE II

Percentage by Occupations, Total and Experimental Groups

Occupations and Professions	Per cent for all 5th and 6th grade pupils combined	Per cent for experimental group
Skilled laborers and tradesmen	31.91	26.67
Faculty members	17.02	23.33
Clerks, salesmen and solicitors	11.35	13.33
Police, firemen, mail-carriers, motormen and conductors	10.64	10.00
Farmers and dairymen	7.80	0.00
Bankers and merchants	6.38	10.00
Unskilled laborers	4.96	0.00
Laundresses, seamstresses and domestics	3.55	6.67
Editors, clergymen, lawyers and physicians	3.55	10.00
Contractors	2.84	0.00

It is here shown that the children from faculty homes furnished somewhat more than their share of the experimental group, since 17 per cent of the total membership of the two grades has supplied 23⅓ per cent of the enrollment of the special room. Again, if to these there are added those children who come from homes representing the other professions, we find that a few more than one-fifth of the total group furnish exactly one-third of the selected upper group.

While this is not sufficient ground for generalization, it is true that under the conditions of this experiment, children from homes representing the so-called learned professions stand a better chance of high rank in school success, as measured by the ordinary methods.

School History

The school progress of most of these children, prior to their enrollment in the experimental room, had been entirely normal; most of them began school at six years of age, or thereabouts, and, with a few exceptions, made a school grade each year after. Only one case of repeating a grade was reported, namely, Number 4, who spent two years in the first grade. Numbers 16 and 26 skipped the third grade, and Numbers 8 and 23 entered the public schools in the third grade, for the former did the work of the first two years at home, and the latter had attended a private school. Number 5 did the work of the first two grades in one year, Number 10 spent only one half-year in the first grade, Number 6 lost half of the second year's work, because of illness, and for that reason has been in school one-half year longer than the normal number of years for reaching the fifth grade; Number 7 missed about half the first year, for the same reason, but did not spend any time in making it up, and hence was not delayed in her progress. Attention should be called to the fact that, measured in terms of time spent in school, but few of these children have derived any advantage from the excellent character of their work, for in only four or five cases has the school made any provision whereby progress more rapid than that of the average child might be made possible for them.

Mental Age

In order to determine the degree of intelligence possessed by each of the members of the experimental group, early in the year they were tested by Miss Coy by the Stanford Revision of the Binet-Simon scale for the Measurement of Intelligence.[1] The results are exhibited in Table III.

[1] Terman, L. M. *The Measurement of Intelligence.*

TABLE III

Mental Age, Advancement, and Intelligence Quotient

Grade	No. Sex	Date of Examination	Chronological Age* Yrs.	Chronological Age* Mos.	Mental Age Yrs.	Mental Age Mos.	Advancement Yrs.	Advancement Mos.	Intelligence Quotient
V.	1. Girl	Oct. 16	10	1	13	11	3	10	138.0
	2. Girl	Oct. 12	10	0	14	8	4	8	146.6
	3. Girl	Sept. 29	10	3	11	3	1	0	110.0
	4. Boy	Oct. 18	11	0	11	2		2	101.5
	5. Girl	Oct. 16	10	7	11	3		8	107.0
	6. Girl	Oct. 2	10	5	13	2	2	9	126.4
	7. Girl	Oct. 13	10	3	11	10	1	7	115.4
	8. Boy	Oct. 17	10	3	12	7	2	4	122.7
	9. Girl	Oct. 23	11	1	12	0		11	108.2
	10. Girl	Oct. 20	9	10	11	7	1	9	117.9
	11. Girl	Oct. 13	10	3	14	6	4	3	141.4
	12. Boy	Oct. 17	11	1	13	5	2	4	121.0
	13. Girl	Oct. 11	10	1	10	3		2	101.6
	14. Boy	Oct. 24	10	3	13	5	3	2	130.9
	15. Boy	Oct. 5	10	10	11	11	1	1	110.0
VI.	16. Boy	Oct. 4	10	4	13	9	3	5	133.0
	17. Boy	Sept. 28	12	1	14	9	2	8	122.0
	18. Girl	Oct. 6	11	7	12	5		10	107.0
	19. Girl	Oct. 3	11	2	13	11	2	9	124.6
	20. Boy	Oct. 6	11	4	11	9		5	103.6
	21. Girl	Sept. 29	12	3	13	1		10	107.0
	22. Boy	Oct. 4	11	7	12	6		11	108.0
	23. Girl	Oct. 2	9	7	12	9	3	2	133.0
	24. Boy	Oct. 9	11	7	11	6		1	99.3
	25. Girl	Sept. 28	11	4	12	5	1	1	110.0
	26. Boy	Oct. 9	10	7	12	7	2	0	118.8
	27. Girl	Sept. 28	11	4	12	10	1	6	113.0
	28. Girl	Oct. 10	10	10	12	6	1	8	115.3
	29. Boy	Oct. 3	11	0	12	2	1	2	110.6
	30. Boy	Oct. 10	12	1	16	1	4	0	134.4

* The chronological age has in each case been calculated to the nearest full month.

By the intelligence quotient (I.Q) is meant the ratio between the mental age of the child, as determined by the Binet scale, and the chronological age. It is found by dividing the mental age by the chronological age. Terman classifies intelligence quotients above 140 as representing "near" genius or genius; those from 120 to 140 as degrees of very superior intelligence; from 110 to 120 as superior intelligence; and from 90 to 110 as normal, or average intelligence. It must be remembered, however, that on account of the impossibility of drawing sharp border-lines these classifications are only approximate.[2] The following table distributes the intelligence quotients shown in the table above into these groups.

TABLE IV

Distribution by Intelligence Groups

	Fifth Grade	Sixth Grade	Total
Normal, or average intelligence.............	6	6	12
Superior intelligence......................	2	4	6
Very superior intelligence..................	5	5	10
Near genius or genius......................	2	0	2

To put the matter in another way, an I. Q. of 110 is equaled or excelled by 20 children out of 100; an I. Q. of 115 by ten out of 100, an I. Q. of 125 by one out of 100, while only about one child in 250 or 300 tests as high as 140.[3] The number of children in the experimental room who reached each of these points is shown in Table V.

TABLE V

Number of Pupils Reaching Higher Intelligence Quotients

I. Q. Reached or Exceeded	Fifth Grade	Sixth Grade	Total	Part of Total School Population Normally Represented
110	10	10	20	Upper 20%
115	8	7	15	Upper 10%
120	7	5	12	Upper 5%
125	5	3	8	Upper 3%
130	4	3	7	Upper 1%
140	2	0	2	Upper 0.3%

It has been suggested that the intelligence standard for admission to a special class for gifted children be set at a mental advancement of two whole years,[4] which, at the age of most of the children in this class, would result in an intelligence quotient of about 120, which Terman makes the dividing line between "superior" and "very superior" intelligence. There are 13 children in the class who show a

[2] Terman, L. M. *Op. cit.*, p. 79.

[3] Terman, L. M. *Op. cit.*, pp. 78, 96.

[4] Hoke, K. J. The Public Schools and the Abnormal Child. *Psychological Clinic*, 9: January, 1916, 238–245.

Goddard, H. H. Two thousand normal children measured by the Binet measuring scale of intelligence. *Pedagogical Seminary* 18: June, 1911, 232–259.

mental advancement of two years or more, and 12 who have an intelligence quotient of 120 or better (Table V). Of these 12, it is interesting to note that four come from the homes of skilled laborers and tradesmen, four are children of bankers or merchants, one comes from the home of a faculty member, two from homes representing other professions, and one from the home of a seamstress. Seven children of faculty members, in the whole group, contribute only one intelligence quotient above 120, although only two of them fall below 110.

Criticism of the Method of Selection

The basis of selection of the pupils of the experimental room and the manner in which that selection was made have been described in an earlier portion of the present chapter. It will be remembered that the room, as actually constituted, received the upper 20 per cent each of the fifth and sixth grades of the Leal School, and that the selection was made entirely upon the opinions of the principal and the teachers, whose judgment, naturally enough, was based largely upon the school records of the individual pupils. It will be seen, however, that in our experimental class we have a very liberal selection, with a consequently wide range of intelligence quotients. Only 12 of the 30 children reach or exceed an I. Q. which entitles them to be classed as possessing "very superior" intelligence, and ten of them are of no better than average, though many of these latter are near the upper limit of that classification. Had the pupils for this room been chosen by means of the results of the mental tests, therefore, there would have been a much better selection, and even more could have been accomplished than actually was.

The tables in the following chapters, which exhibit the results of the various educational and psychological tests that were used, show a comparatively wide range of ability in each test, even in the selected group. This is owing chiefly to the fact that one or two individuals, whose intelligence quotients are the lowest in the room, are also consistently low in the tests. A better method of selection would have eliminated these pupils and thus made possible more uniform results. Our experience throughout the year indicated very strongly that the selection of pupils for a special room for gifted children should be made by means of psychological tests, rather than being allowed to depend upon the opinions of teachers and principals, or even upon the record of the teachers' marks secured by the child in the various school subjects.[5]

Amount of Work Accomplished

An important part of the experiment consisted in keeping a close comparison of the progress of the special room with that of the other rooms of the same grade. It will be remembered that the special room was not established until October 2nd, or three weeks after the work of the school year had begun. During those three weeks the pupils who had been selected, carried on their work in the regular rooms with the rest of the class, and in that way, from the point of view of the experimental work, some time was lost. At the end of November, that is to say, in eight weeks, a careful account was taken of the work which had been done in the different rooms, and it was found that the special 5th grade group had accomplished approximately 50 per cent more work than the regular 5th grades had done in arithmetic, 100 per cent more in language, and 50 per cent more in geography. The 6th grade, in amount of work done, had made a gain of approximately 75 per cent in arithmetic and 66 per cent in language. Besides this, both grades in the room had finished the half-year's work in physiology prescribed by the course of study, and had begun upon the work in history which regularly follows the completion of the work in physiology, as the course is arranged. Final examinations in arithmetic, set by the city superintendent and covering the work of a whole school year for each grade, *i.e.*, those regularly given in June, were given to both grades on February 9, 1917, and the corresponding examinations in language were given one week later. The 5th grade took the final examination in geography on February 19. All these examinations were under the supervision of the superintendent, and the papers, after having been graded by the teacher, were sent to his office for inspection and approval. In each case the results were satisfactory, and the classes were allowed to go on at once with the work of the next year in the respective branches. The Urbana course of study provides for only two months' work in geography for the 6th grade, beginning

[5] For an extended discussion of this matter, see G. M. Whipple, *Classes for Gifted Children*, Bloomington, Ill., 1919.

April first. With this 6th grade, however, the work was begun after the Christmas vacation and was completed by the end of February, at which time the 7th grade work in the same subject was undertaken. At the end of the school year both grades had completed another year of work, with the exception of the work in history, in which, for various reasons, mainly because of difficulty in articulating the work of the Special Room with the course of study used in the Urbana school system, as required by the superintendent, and therefore beyond our control, they still lacked a few weeks' work. During the first week in June, 1917, the children of the Special Group were given the regular final examinations in the subjects of the 6th and 7th grades as outlined for the other rooms, with the understanding that if these examinations were passed, and the deficiencies in history made up during the summer months, or in the following year, they would be permitted to enter the grade ahead at the beginning of the next school year, in this way making a gain of one year. Nine pupils of the Special Fifth, and eight of the Special Sixth passed the examinations and received certificates of promotion. A number of the children failed in the examination in arithmetic, the papers from which were scored by the superintendent himself, and that in a very rigorous way. Almost all the members of this latter group did review work in arithmetic during the summer and passed a special examination set for them in September, thus gaining promotion. It should be noted, in this connection, that the matter of the promotion of the pupils of the Special Group rested entirely with the decision of the superintendent.[6] In addition, it may be said that practically all of those who failed to receive promotion either in June or in September would never had been admitted to the Special Group if the selection had been made by the use of our psychological tests, rather than upon the single basis of teachers' judgments.

Health

The extra amount of work which the pupils carried resulted in no case in any impairment of health. Careful watch was kept for any symptoms of nerve strain, or any other indications of weakness, but nothing of the sort was detected. Two children put on eye-

[6] For a detailed account of this phase of the investigation, see Whipple, *op. cit.*, pp. 83–93

glasses early in the year, and in consequence of advice given them as the result of tests of vision, rather than because of any extra strain. Careful inspection was made of the children's teeth by a competent dentist, and a copy of his report transmitted to the parents.

Attendance

In regularity of attendance, the experimental room surpassed the other rooms of the same grade which were in the building. Table VI shows the per cent of attendance for all rooms in the Leal School enrolling 5th and 6th grade pupils, by months from October, 1916, to March, 1917, inclusive. September, 1916, is omitted for the reason that the special room was not in existence during that month.

TABLE VI

Per Cent of Attendance by Months

	Oct.	Nov.	Dec.	Jan.	Feb.	Mar.	Average
Room 5Y.........	97.5	95.5	96.8	93.8	93.1	95.3	95.83
Room 5-6F.......	98.3	96.7	96.2	96.5	94.1	94.6	96.07
Room 6G.........	98.9	97.5	96.3	96.3	96.7	97.6	97.19
Experimental Room	99.1	98.7	99.7	98.8	99.0	99.1	99.07

Atmosphere

The 'atmosphere' of the room throughout the whole year was entirely normal. Although it is sometimes urged as an argument against the establishment of special rooms for gifted children that there is danger of the development of egotism, clannishness, or similar undesirable characteristics on the part of children placed in such rooms, the pupils under observation did not exhibit any inordinate amount of any such traits. They enjoy the opportunity of using their powers, and such was their industry and their interest in their work that discipline was reduced to a minimum, and the teacher left free to spend all her energies in the work of instruction.

Summary

In summary of this chapter it may be said that, in so far as the conditions of the experiment may be considered as typical, children from the top fifth of the 5th and 6th grades of the elementary school, selected, in general, on the basis of the ordinary tests of school work, are in median age from two to six months younger than the children composing the remaining four-fifths. They are somewhat more likely to come from the homes of professional fathers than from the homes of skilled or unskilled laborers. But few of them derive any advantage, in terms of school progress, from the excellence of their work, although from one-third to one-half of them are advanced in mental age two years beyond their chronological age, and possess a degree of intelligence enabling them to be classed intellectually as "very superior." Children falling within this latter group, which includes practically the top ten per cent, are able to do approximately two years of the work outlined in the ordinary course of study for the middle- and lower-grammar grades in one year, with a degree of excellence fully up to the standard, and without any undue strain or impairment of health. They excel ordinary children in regularity of attendance, are not abnormally clannish or selfish, are industrious and cause practically no trouble in discipline.

CHAPTER IV

RESULTS OF THE EDUCATIONAL TESTS

In order to determine the efficiency in the fundamental branches of the special room as a whole, as well as to ascertain the points of strength or weakness in each pupil individually, throughout the year use was made of the various educational scales and tests for ability in handwriting, spelling, arithmetic, and composition; while other tests, not quite so closely connected with some particular branch, were used to test different types of language ability. It was possible, by comparing the results of these tests with the norms established for them, to determine what degree of efficiency the room had attained. In some instances these tests were given to the other rooms in the building which were cited in the previous chapter as "control groups,"[1] and this made possible a direct comparison of the efficiency of the special room with that of the rest of the school. We shall proceed at once to set forth the results of these tests for the various studies.

Handwriting

To determine the quality of handwriting, samples were secured in the experimental room on October third, the second day the room was in session. These samples were scored on both the Ayres[2] and the Thorndike scales[3] for the measurement of ability in handwriting, by sixteen graduate students in education. Table VII shows the median and the average amalgamated score on each scale for each grade. It also shows the range of the median score for each grade among the sixteen persons who did the scoring. The samples were scored for quality only; no account was taken of speed.

[1] See Chapter III.

[2] Ayres, L. P. *A Scale for Measuring the Quality of Handwriting of School Children.*

[3] Thorndike, E. L. *A Scale for Handwriting of Children in Grades 5 to 8.*

Thorndike, E. L. The measurement of the quality of handwriting. *Teachers College Record*, 11: March, 1910, 83–175.

TABLE VII

Quality of Handwriting Produced by Pupils of Special Room, October 3, 1916. Ayres and Thorndike Scales, 16 Judges

	FIFTH GRADE		SIXTH GRADE	
	Thorndike	Ayres	Thorndike	Ayres
Median	9.8	48.6	10.4	49.5
Average	10.0	48.6	10.5	50.8
Median Range	8.5–11.5	36.8–61.8	7.6–12.9	29.7–71.5

Starch's standard scores (Table VIII), are based on over 6,000 pupils in 28 schools, and apply to the ends of the respective years.[4]

TABLE VIII

Quality of Handwriting. Standard Scores for End of Each Grade, Ayres and Thorndike Scales (Starch)

GRADES	4	5	6	7	8
Quality (Thorndike)	8.7	9.3	9.8	10.4	10.9
Quality (Ayres)	37	43	53	57	....

A comparison of Tables VII and VIII shows that, taking the median scores on the Thorndike scale, the fifth grade has attained a quality equal to the standard score at the end of the sixth grade, while the sixth grade has reached the ability to be expected at the end of the seventh grade. Since the samples were taken at the beginning of the year, or only three weeks after the beginning, to be exact, the scores must be considered as representing the ability possessed by these pupils at the end of the fourth and fifth grades. In other words, they must be compared not with the fifth-grade and sixth-grade scores, but with those of a year earlier. Consequently, accepting Starch's scores as the true norms, and considering the judging as efficient, on the basis of the Thorndike scale the median score of each grade is two years ahead of what it might be expected to be. The same statement is true when we use the average instead of the median, for in both grades the average is slightly the higher of the two measures.

[4] Starch, D. *Educational Measurements*, pp. 82–83.

With the Ayres scale, the results are slightly different. The average score for the fifth grade stands just a trifle above the mid-point between the standard scores at the ends of the fifth and sixth grades. If we could assume that the difference between the standard scores for these grades represented ten equal steps on the scale, then our fifth-grade group would fall at a point representing about the middle of the sixth grade, with the sixth-grade group slightly above it. Remembering again that our groups are at the beginning of the year, this calculation would show the fifth-grade group advanced one and one-half years in average score, and the sixth-grade group advanced one-half year. Without going into the argument as to the relative merits of these two scales, it seems safe to assume that the experimental group, in terms of average score, is advanced at least one year in average quality of handwriting.

SPELLING

For testing ability in spelling, three of the lists in Ayres's scale for Spelling[5] were used; List N. given on October 2, List R, given October 20, and List U, given October 30. Table IX exhibits the average, the median, and the range of the percentage of words of each list spelled correctly by each of the two grades.

TABLE IX

Percentage of Words Spelled Correctly. Lists N, R, U, Ayres' Spelling Scale

List	Grade	Median	Average	Range
N.	5	92.00	91.52	70.13–98.70
	6	97.52	97.27	92.21–100.0
R.	5	80.80	73.21	25.00–98.21
	6	93.03	91.43	64.29–98.21
U.	5	48.53	50.00	9.67–76.47
	6	75.00	75.29	29.41–97.06

In Table X we have the standard percentages for each list, by grades, from data furnished by Ayres.

[5] Ayres, L. P. *A Measuring Scale for Ability in Spelling.*

TABLE X

Standard Percentages of Words Spelled Correctly by Grades, Lists N, R, U, Ayres' Spelling Scale (After Ayres)

Grade	List N	List R	List U
4	77–81	46–54	.....
5	87–90	63–69	.....
6	94–95	77–81	55–62
7	98	87–90	70–76
8	100	94–95	82–86

Accepting the median as the truer measure of the central tendency, which it probably is in this case (although the difference between median and average assumes importance only with List R, especially in the fifth grade), we have, by combining Tables IX and X, a table which shows us the grade of spelling ability reached by the median score and range of each grade.

TABLE XI

Grade of Spelling Ability Reached or Exceeded by Median and Extreme Scores of Each Grade in Experimental Room. Lists N, R, U, Ayres' Spelling Scale

List	Grade	Grade Reached by Median Score	Grades Reached by Extreme Scores	
			Lowest	Highest
N	5	5.5	3	7
	6	7.0	5	8
R	5	6.00	3	8
	6	7.75	5	8
U	5	*	*	6
	6	7	*	8

* No standards for corresponding scores given in this list.

It will be seen, upon examination of Table XI, that each of the grades in the special room had reached a degree of spelling ability approximately equal to that of the grade above it. The difference is more marked than it appears to be, when we take into consideration the fact that these lists were given at the beginning of the year, and it is, therefore, a very conservative estimate to say that the selected pupils are as a group one year advanced in spelling ability.

With the idea that a more rigorous test of spelling than the Ayres scale should be employed to obtain valid results, the superintendent of schools, during the first week in April, 1917, gave Lists Three and Four of Starch's tests in spelling[6] to all the 5th and 6th-grade pupils in the building. The average percentage of words spelled correctly, by grades and rooms, was as shown in Table XII.

TABLE XII

Percentage of Words Spelled Correctly by Fifth and Sixth Grade Pupils. Starch's Spelling Tests, Lists III and IV

Room and Grade *	Per Cent
5 F	68.13
5 Y	61.50
5 Exp	71.30
6 F	69.68
6 G	72.02
6 Exp	79.05

* It will be noted that this table includes Rooms 5-6 F, 5 Y, and 6 G, which have already been described as forming a control group. See Chapter III.

Starch gives as standards for each grade the percentages indicated in Table XIII.

TABLE XIII

Standard Scores. Starch's Spelling Test

Grades	V	VI	VII	VIII
Percentage of Words Correct	61	71	78	85

By comparing our results with the standard scores, we find that the experimental fifth grade, which at the time of the test, had really become a sixth grade in respect to the work it was doing, was up to the 6th-grade standard in spelling ability. Likewise, the special 6th grade, then virtually doing 7th-grade work, was up to the standard for that grade. Of the control groups, all were up to grade, or better, with the exception of the class designated as 6 F, which was a little below the standard for its grade. The results of the Starch tests, then, corroborated those obtained earlier in the year with the Ayres test and confirmed the assertion of the investigators that the selected pupils, were, as a group, distinctly superior in ability to spell.

Arithmetic

Several different methods of testing arithmetical abilities were used during the year. To determine efficiency in the four funda-

[6] Starch, D. *Educational Measurements*, pp. 88–98.

mentals, the Woody Arithmetic Scales, Series A, were used.[7] This series consists of a set of four graded scales, one for each of the fundamental operations. They were given to the pupils of the experimental room on the dates indicated in Table XIV, in the manner prescribed by their author, and the class score in each of the operations was calculated according to his directions. This score represents the degree of difficulty on the scale of that problem which could be solved with absolute accuracy by just 50 per cent of the class.

TABLE XIV

Class Scores, Experimental Room, Woody Arithmetic Scales, Series A

		Fifth Grade	Sixth Grade
Addition	Nov. 7	8.18	8.39
Subtraction	Nov. 10	6.91	7.55
Multiplication	Nov. 13	6.37	7.39
Division	Nov. 14	6.14	7.34

Woody gives the figures shown in Table XV as the tentative standards of achievement in these scales, when the tests are given during the first part of the school year. They are, then, directly comparable with our scores.

TABLE XV

Tentative Standards of Achievement, Woody Arithmetic Scales, Series A

Grade	Addition	Subtraction	Multiplicat'n	Division
V	6.99	5.47	5.53	4.94
VI	7.95	6.46	6.72	5.87
VII	8.65	7.31	7.26	6.59
VIII	9.01	7.64	7.93	7.16

Comparing our class scores with these tentative standards, we find that our fifth grade excels the 6th-grade standard in addition, subtraction, and division, and almost reaches it in multiplication; while our sixth grade, although not quite reaching the 7th-grade standard in addition, goes beyond it in subtraction and multiplication, and excels the 8th-grade standard in division.

As the Woody scales were originally published, they consisted of two series of four scales each, so that each scale tested ability in only one of the fundamentals. A modification of them has since been published, consisting of two sheets of problems, representing

[7] Woody, C. *Measurements of Some Achievements in Arithmetic.* Teachers College, Columbia University Contributions to Education, No. 80, pp. 3–22.

all four of the fundamental operations upon one scale.[8] Since norms for the scales in this form have not yet been published, we gave them not only to the pupils of the experimental room, but also to those other rooms of the same grade in the building that afforded the control group already described. Scale I was given in all the rooms on February 1. Scale II was given to the control rooms on February 9, and to the experimental room on February 12. The results have been scored in two ways: (1) by finding the number of problems correctly solved within the time-limit of 20 minutes, and (2) by computing the time in seconds required for one correct solution. Tables XVI–XIX show these scores for each scale.

TABLE XVI

Woody-McCall Arithmetic Scales, Mixed Fundamentals, B I. Number Correct Solutions in Twenty Minutes

Number Correct	NUMBER OF PUPILS					
	Fifth Grade			Sixth Grade		
	Total	Control	Selected	Total	Control	Selected
14	.....	1	0	.....	0	0
15	.....	0	0	.....	0	0
16	.....	0	0	.....	0	0
17	.....	1	0	.....	1	0
18	.....	2	0	.....	0	0
19	.....	3	0	.....	1	0
20	.....	2	0	.....	1	0
21	.....	3	1	.....	2	0
22	.....	5	0	.....	2	0
23	.....	3	1	.....	6	0
24	.....	13	0	.....	8	1
25	.....	8	4	.....	4	1
26	.....	5	2	.....	4	2
27	.....	1	0	.....	7	1
28	.....	2	4	.....	7	3
29	.....	2	0	.....	6	0
30	.....	0	2	.....	4	3
31	.....	0	0	.....	2	1
32	.....	0	0	.....	0	3
33	.....	0	0	.....	1	0
Sum	.....	51	14	.....	56	15
Group:						
Median	24.85	24.46	26.25	25.84	26.25	28.84
Average	23.95	23.31	26.34	25.09	24.10	28.60
Range	14–30	14–29	21–30	17–33	17–33	24–32

[8] *Woody-McCall Arithmetic Scales, Mixed Fundamentals,* Series B, I and II.

TABLE XVII

Woody-McCall Arithmetic Scales, Mixed Fundamentals, B I. Time Required for One Correct Solution

Time in Seconds	Number of Pupils					
	Fifth Grade			Sixth Grade		
	Total	Control	Selected	Total	Control	Selected
84–82	.....	1	0	.....	0	0
81–79	.....	0	0	.....	0	0
78–76	.....	0	0	.....	0	0
75–73	.....	0	0	.....	0	0
72–70	.....	1	0	.....	1	0
69–67	.....	1	0	.....	0	0
66–64	.....	1	0	.....	0	0
63–61	.....	2	0	.....	0	0
60–58	.....	3	0	.....	2	0
57–58	.....	6	1	.....	3	0
54–52	.....	3	0	.....	4	0
51–49	.....	13	0	.....	9	0
48–46	.....	11	3	.....	7	1
45–43	.....	5	4	.....	14	0
42–40	.....	2	1	.....	9	1
39–37	.....	2	0	.....	3	2
36–34	.....	0	2	.....	2	0
33–31	.....	0	1	.....	2	3
30–28	.....	0	2	.....	0	4
27–25	.....	0	0	.....	0	2
24–22	.....	0	0	.....	0	2
Sum	.....	51	14	.....	56	15
Group:						
Median	48.42	50.00	43.25	43.50	44.43	30.25
Average	49.35	51.60	41.11	43.00	46.03	31.70
Range	83.6–30.2	83.6–35.2	57.2–30.2	70.6–23.3	70.6–31.9	48.0–2.33

TABLE XVIII

Woody-McCall Arithmetic Scales, Mixed Fundamentals, B II. Number Correct Solutions in Twenty Minutes

Number Correct	NUMBER OF PUPILS					
	Fifth Grade			Sixth Grade		
	Total	Control	Selected	Total	Control	Selected
13	.....	3	0	.....	0	0
14	.....	0	0	.....	0	0
15	.....	0	0	.....	0	0
16	.....	0	0	.....	0	0
17	.....	1	0	.....	0	0
18	.....	2	0	.....	0	0
19	.....	0	0	.....	0	0
20	.....	1	0	.....	0	0
21	.....	2	0	.....	4	0
22	.....	4	0	.....	3	0
23	.....	6	0	.....	3	0
24	.....	10	2	.....	7	0
25	.....	8	1	.....	3	1
26	.....	6	2	.....	7	0
27	.....	4	2	.....	7	3
28	.....	1	2	.....	5	3
29	.....	5	3	.....	1	1
30	.....	0	1	.....	4	2
31	.....	0	2	.....	6	2
32	.....	0	0	.....	5	1
33	.....	0	0	.....	2	2
Sum	.....	53	15	.....	57	15
Group:						
Median	25.39	24.75	28.25	27.85	27.28	29.50
Average	24.57	23.71	27.60	27.15	26.59	29.26
Range	13–31	13–39	24–31	21–33	21–33	25–33

TABLE XIX

Woody-McCall Arithmetic Scales, Mixed Fundamentals, B II. Time Required for One Correct Solution

Time in Seconds	Number of Pupils					
	Fifth Grade			Sixth Grade		
	Total	Control	Selected	Total	Control	Selected
93–91	.....	2	0	.....	0	0
90–88	.....	0	0	.....	0	0
87–85	.....	0	0	.....	0	0
84–82	.....	0	0	.....	0	0
81–79	.....	0	0	.....	0	0
78–76	.....	0	0	.....	0	0
75–73	.....	1	0	.....	0	0
72–70	.....	1	0	.....	0	0
69–67	.....	0	0	.....	0	0
66–64	.....	0	0	.....	0	0
63–61	.....	1	0	.....	0	0
60–58	.....	1	0	.....	0	0
57–55	.....	3	0	.....	2	0
54–52	.....	1	0	.....	2	0
51–49	.....	3	0	.....	3	0
48–46	.....	7	0	.....	1	0
45–43	.....	6	0	.....	6	0
42–40	.....	5	2	.....	3	0
39–37	.....	2	0	.....	6	0
36–34	.....	5	3	.....	4	1
33–31	.....	4	1	.....	11	1
30–28	.....	6	5	.....	5	0
27–25	.....	5	2	.....	8	4
24–22	.....	0	1	.....	5	4
21–19	.....	0	1	.....	1	4
18–16	.....	0	0	.....	0	0
15–13	.....	0	0	.....	0	1
Sum	.....	53	15	.....	57	15
Group:						
Median	39.00	42.20	29.25	31.40	33.00	22.33
Average	40.69	43.50	30.70	34.16	35.37	23.80
Range	92.3–20.4	92.3–24.8	40–20.4	54.5–14.5	54.5–20.6	35.2–14.5

An examination of these tables reveals a marked superiority of the pupils of the special room over those of the same grades in the regular rooms. On Scale I, the median score for number of correct solutions in 20 minutes is, for the special fifth grade, almost two problems better than the median for the 5th-grade control group, and the difference is over two problems in case of the two 6th-grade groups. On Scale II, the special fifth grade exceeds its control group in median score by three and one-half problems, and the corresponding difference in favor of the special 6th grade is practically two and one-fourth problems. If the averages are taken instead of the medians, all these differences are materially increased.

In the score by time required for one correct solution, Scale I, the special 5th-grade's median time is shorter by 6.75 seconds than that of its control group, and the special 6th grade is faster than its control group by over 14 seconds. For Scale II, the corresponding differences are 13 seconds (nearly) and 10.66 seconds. For both scales, and by both methods of scoring, in every case the median score of the special 5th-grade group reaches or exceeds the median score of the 6th-grade control group, and in every case but one (Table XVII) it exceeds that of the total 6th-grade group.

Bonser's tests for mathematical judgment[9] were given to the different rooms early in March. These consist of two sets of five two-step problems, stated in the usual textbook form (Test I, A and B), and two sets of five problems of the same difficulty as the preceding, so far as the processes which are involved are concerned, but stated in a less familiar way (Test II, A and B). Bonser says that Tests I and II test mathematical judgment, or, in general, that form of deductive reasoning of the usual scientific type, involving data, principles, and inferences. In giving them, when the first pupil to finish had completed his work, all turned the papers face downward, and they were collected. They were given first in the experimental room, and the time-limit for each grade in the control room was fixed at the number of seconds it took the first child in that grade in the special room to finish. This made the time in the fifth grade for List I A, 108 seconds; for List I B, 94 seconds; for List II A, 107 seconds; and for List II B, 64 seconds. The corresponding time-limits in the sixth grade were 103, 82, 73, and 64 seconds, respectively. In scoring the papers, Bonser's directions were followed, so that a grade of 2 was given for each correct solution of a problem in arithmetic. If one part of a two-step problem was right, and the other not, a grade of 1 was given. No deductions were made for inaccuracies in operations. In the accompanying table the scores of the four different lists have been combined, by adding, into one score for all.

[9] Bonser, F. G. *The Reasoning Ability of Children of the Fourth, Fifth, and Sixth School Grades.* Teachers College, Columbia University Contributions to Education, No. 37, pp. 2, 10, 14, 16.

TABLE XX

Bonser's Reasoning Tests I and II. (Mathematical Judgment)

Score	Number of Pupils					
	Fifth Grade			Sixth Grade		
	Total	Control	Selected	Total	Control	Selected
0	.....	5	0	.....	3	0
1–2	.....	7	0	.....	7	0
3–4	.....	6	2	.....	10	0
5–6	.....	7	0	.....	6	0
7–8	.....	7	2	.....	3	2
9–10	.....	2	2	.....	10	1
11–12	.....	5	1	.....	2	1
13–14	.....	1	1	.....	5	0
15–16	.....	2	1	.....	2	2
17–18	.....	1	3	.....	4	1
19–20	.....	1	2	.....	2	0
21–22	.....	1	0	.....	1	1
23–24	.....	1	0	.....	5	2
25–26	.....	1	0	.....	0	2
27–28	.....	0	0	.....	0	2
29–30	.....	0	1	.....	0	0
31–32	.....	0	0	.....	0	0
33–34	.....	0	0	.....	0	0
35–36	.....	0	0	.....	0	0
37–38	.....	0	0	.....	0	0
39–40	.....	0	0	.....	0	1
Sum	.....	47	15	.....	60	15
Group:						
Median	8.25	6.7	14.5	10.59	10.15	22.50
Average	9.19	7.7	13.89	11.88	9.78	20.27
Range	0–30	0–25	4–30	0–39	0–24	8–39

Here again, as with the tests in fundamentals, the selected group is far superior to the control group, and it is likewise again true that the median and average score for the special 5th grade exceed the median and average of the whole group of 6th-grade pupils, when those in the special room are not treated separately.

Language

The first of the several tests of language ability which were used was Winch's test for the invention of stories. This test is fully described in Whipple's *Manual* (Part II, p. 269), and may be regarded as putting a premium upon literary ability, or constructive imagination in the field of words. In giving it, there was presented to each subject a sheet of paper at the top of which were printed ten words, with the instruction to write a story in which each of these ten words should be used. No time-limit was imposed. This test was given only to the special room, and was given twice. On October 31, the following list of words was used: *orphan, garden, hungry, station, parents, clothing, visitor, cottage, train, country;* on November 3 the test was repeated, with the following words: *snowstorm, children, ticket, clock, dog, screams, church, basket, river, ice.* The stories which the pupils wrote were graded by 17 graduate students in education, using the Hillegas-Thorndike scale for the measurement of quality in English composition,[10] with the results which are shown in Table XXI.

TABLE XXI

Quality of Composition (16 Judges)

		"Orphan" List	"Snowstorm" List
Fifth Grade	Median	37.8	37.7
	Average	38.02	39.42
	Range	27.7–47.6	28.4–49.1
Sixth Grade	Median	47.2	45.6
	Average	47.8	44.1
	Range	33.7–63.0	28.6–62.5

Starch[11] publishes standards for the Hillegas-Thorndike scale, derived from the ratings of compositions written by over 5,000 pupils, including the reports of the Butte, Montana, and Salt Lake City, Utah, surveys. Trabue, as a result of his investigations of composition tests and measurements in a number of typical school systems, including those mentioned above, has proposed tentative standard medians, showing the quality of compositions to be expected from at least half of a normal class at the end of any given school year.[12] These proposed standards are higher than the majority of the schools in Trabue's list have actually achieved, although at each grade at least one school has excelled the standard. Both Starch's and Trabue's standards are given in Table XXII.

[10] Thorndike, E. L. *Preliminary Extension of the Hillegas Scale for the Measurement of Quality in English Composition by Young People.*

[11] Starch, D. *Educational Measurements*, p. 145.

[12] Trabue, M. R. Supplementing the Hillegas Scale. *Teachers College Record*, 18: 51–84.

TABLE XXII

Standard Scores for the Hillegas-Thorndike Scale (After Starch and Trabue)

Grades	IV	V	VI	VII	VIII
Standards (Starch)	26	31	36	41	46
Standards (Trabue)	35	40	45	50	55

By comparing our results with these scores, it will be seen that our special 5th-grade pupils at the beginning of the year had reached a standard of quality in English composition almost equal to Starch's 7th-grade standard, and that the 6th-grade, if we take the mean of the two tests, had 8th-grade ability at that time. By Trabue's standards, which are admittedly somewhat higher than those found in practice, the 5th grade at the beginning of the year had practically that degree of ability to be expected from them at the close of the year, and the same thing is true of the sixth grade.

It must be remembered, however, that in giving a list of ten words which must be used in these stories, a factor was introduced which would not have to be reckoned with in rating compositions written under ordinary circumstances. Just what the effect of this factor would be, is difficult to determine; it is a question whether compositions thus written would grade higher or lower on the scale than those written under a set subject. I am inclined to think, however, that furnishing the list of words tended to raise the quality of the composition, and that, therefore, our scores are just a little too high to be a fair measure of the ability of these pupils in composition. The words that were given in the test probably suggested a plot and made for a coherent development that otherwise might not have been obtained. On the other hand, there was the disadvantage of loss of freedom and initiative, with the consequent creation of a somewhat artificial situation.

Trabue's Language Scales

In Trabue's Completion-Test Language Scales, we have a test for language ability of a different type. These scales represent varieties of the well-known completion method, or completion tests, which consist of a series of sentences in which certain words are elided. The task is to fill each blank with a single word that makes sense. There is evidence that there is a rather high positive correlation between ability in Trabue's tests and ability in other tests of language and also general intelligence. Scales B and C of these tests were given to the special room in the latter part of October, and to the control rooms about the middle of December. They were given and scored in exact accordance with Trabue's directions.[13] For our purposes, the scores for the two tests have been combined, by adding, into a single score. The scores thus obtained are displayed in Table XXIII.

TABLE XXIII

Combined Scores, Trabue Language Scales B and C

Score	NUMBER OF PUPILS					
	Fifth Grade			Sixth Grade		
	Total	Control	Selected	Total	Control	Selected
12	.....	2	0	.....		0
13	.....	1	0	.....	1	0
14	.....	0	0	.....	0	0
15	.....	0	0	.....	0	0
16	.....	2	0	.....	2	0
17	.....	2	0	.....	1	0
18	.....	0	0	.....	4	0
19	.....	3	0	.....	2	0
20	.....	2	0	.....	4	0
21	.....	3	1	.....	7	1
22	.....	6	1	.....	6	0
23	.....	7	3	.....	5	1
24	.....	2	0	.....	2	1
25	.....	8	0	.....	2	1
26	.....	2	3	.....	6	1
27	.....	0	2	.....	6	5
28	.....	3	1	.....	3	0
29	.....	0	2	.....	2	1
30	.....	1	0	.....	3	1
31	.....	0	0	.....	1	0
32	.....	2	1	.....	1	0
33	.....	0	1	.....	0	0
34	.....	0	0	.....	0	1
35	.....	0	0	.....	0	1
36	.....	0	0	.....	0	1
Sum	.....	46	15	.....	58	15
Group:						
Median	23.80	22.48	26.70	24.83	23.39	27.50
Average	23.25	22.39	26.30	24.32	23.50	27.90
Range	12–33	12–32	21–33	13–36	13–32	21–36

[13] Trabue, M. R. *Completion-Test Language Scales*. Teachers College, Columbia University Contributions to Education, No. 77, especially pp. 19–22, 78–80, 117–118.

In this test, again, the median and average scores attained by the 5th-grade pupils in the special room are above those for the 6th grade of the school, taken as a single group. Trabue gives the following as the tentative standard scores in his Language Scales B, C, D, and E, which, he says, are practically equal in difficulty.

TABLE XXIV

Tentative Standard Scores in Trabue's Language Scales B, C, D, and E (Trabue)

Grade	V	VI	VII	VIII	IX	X	XI	XII
Median................	9.6	11.0	12.3	13.3	14.2	15.3	15.8	16.2

Since in Table XXIII the individual scores represent the sum of the scores in two scales, if we assume those scales to be of equal difficulty, the scores there given may be compared with the standards by dividing them by 2. With that adjustment, it will be seen that the special 5th grade reaches the 8th-grade standard, and the 6th grade almost, though not quite, reaches the 9th-grade. The total 5th-grade group, treated in the mass, excels the 6th-grade standard, and in the same way the total 6th grade goes above the standard proposed for the seventh. Trabue remarks, however, that his proposed standards are more likely to prove too low than too high.

Reading

The reading scales which were used were those devised by Thorndike, namely, his Reading Scale A[14] and Reading Scale Alpha 2.[15] Reading Scale A, or the "visual vocabulary scale," is designed to measure ability in reading words, while Scale Alpha 2 measures ability in paragraph reading. Both scales primarily measure comprehension, leaving speed out of account, although the latter is an important element in reading.

Thorndike Reading Scale A, the visual vocabulary scale, was given to the selected room on October 17, and to the control rooms on January 18, just three months later. This difference in time would work to the disadvantage of the selected pupils, and must be taken into account in comparing their scores with those made by the pupils in the other rooms. By Thorndike's method of scoring, the selected

[14] Thorndike, E. L. The measurement of ability in reading. *Teachers College Record*, 15: September, 1914, 207–277.

[15] Thorndike, E. L. An improved scale for measuring ability in reading. *Teachers College Record*, 16: November, 1915, 31–53.

5th grade attained a class score of 6.38 and the selected 6th grade one of 7.83. Thorndike's standards for this test, by class scores, are for the 5th grade, 5.3; for the 6th, 6.4; for the 7th, 7.1; and for the 8th, 8.2. It will be seen, then, that our 5th grade, shortly after the beginning of the year, had attained practically the 6th-grade standard in this test, while the 6th grade, at the same time, had almost achieved the 8th-grade standard.

In addition to being scored according to Thorndike's directions, this test was also scored by the method of dividing the per cent of accuracy by the time. Table XXV shows the results as scored by the latter method.

TABLE XXV

Thorndike's Reading Scale A, Accuracy Divided by Time

	NUMBER OF PUPILS					
	Fifth Grade			Sixth Grade		
Score*	Total	Control	Selected	Total	Control	Selected
21– 30	.....	1	0	.....	1	0
31– 40	.....	8	0	.....	1	0
41– 50	.....	5	2	.....	2	0
51– 60	.....	5	3	.....	3	0
61– 70	.....	8	1	.....	3	0
71– 80	.....	4	2	.....	7	2
81– 90	.....	6	0	.....	7	0
91–100	.....	3	1	.....	8	0
101–110	.....	2	3	.....	6	1
111–120	.....	2	1	.....	5	1
121–130	.....	1	1	.....	3	1
131–140	.....	5	0	.....	2	2
141–150	.....	1	0	.....	1	1
151–160	.....	0	0	.....	2	1
161–170	.....	0	0	.....	3	2
171–180	.....	0	0	.....	0	0
181–190	.....	0	0	.....	0	1
191–200	.....	0	0	.....	1	1
201–210	.....	0	1	.....	1	0
211–220	.....	0	0	.....	2	0
221–230	.....	0	0	.....	0	0
231–240	.....	0	0	.....	1	0
241–250	.....	0	0	.....	0	1
251–260	.....	0	0	.....	0	0
261–350	.....	0	0	.....	0	0
351–360	.....	0	0	.....	0	1
Sum	.....	51	15	.....	59	15
Group:						
Median	72.5	71.3	78.4	104.3	100.4	147.4
Average	78.5	75.3	89.3	117.2	106.7	158.5
Range	26–204.4	41–204.4	26–145	26–354.5	26–236	78–354.5

* To avoid decimal points, these scores have been multiplied by 100.

Thorndike's Scale Alpha 2 was given in all the rooms at about the middle of February. In scoring the results, only Steps 7 to 9, inclusive, were taken into account. This test was also scored in two ways. The class score for the special 5th grade, computed by Thorndike's methods, was 7.14, and for the 6th it was 7.25. Thorndike's standard for the 5th grade is 5.7; for the 6th, 6.5; for the 7th, 7.0; and for the 8th, 7.5. The special 5th grade, therefore, at the time this test was given, had attained an ability in comprehension of paragraphs some-

TABLE XXVI

Thorndike's Reading Scale Alpha 2, Steps 7 to 9. Scores by Sum of Weighted Answers

	NUMBER OF PUPILS					
	Fifth Grade			Sixth Grade		
Scores	Total	Control	Selected	Total	Control	Selected
11– 15	.....	1	0	.....	0	0
16– 20	.....	0	0	.....	0	0
21– 25	.....	2	0	.....	1	0
26– 30	.....	1	0	.....	0	0
31– 35	.....	0	0	.....	0	0
36– 40	.....	1	0	.....	4	1
41– 45	.....	3	1	.....	1	0
46– 50	.....	3	0	.....	2	0
51– 55	.....	3	0	.....	4	0
56– 60	.....	6	0	.....	4	0
61– 65	.....	4	0	.....	1	0
66– 70	.....	4	1	.....	5	0
71– 75	.....	4	1	.....	7	3
76– 80	.....	3	1	.....	2	1
81– 85	.....	7	0	.....	5	1
86– 90	.....	1	0	.....	0	0
91– 95	.....	2	1	.....	3	1
96–100	.....	2	2	.....	3	0
101–105	.....	0	0	.....	1	0
106–110	.....	4	0	.....	4	0
111–115	.....	0	2	.....	4	1
116–120	.....	0	2	.....	1	3
121–125	.....	0	2	.....	2	0
126–130	.....	0	1	.....	0	1
131–135	.....	0	0	.....	2	1
136–140	.....	0	0	.....	1	0
141–145	.....	0	1	.....	1	0
146–151	.....	0	0	.....	1	2
Sum	.....	51	15	.....	59	15
Group:						
Median	74.5	76.5	112.25	82.25	76.83	113.50
Average	75.63	68.14	101.00	86.96	82.44	102.04
Range	14–141.66	14–108.3	44–141.66	21–149	21–148	39–149

what above the standard to be expected of the 7th grade, while the special 6th grade was a little higher, though not quite up to the 8th-grade standard. Allowing for the fact that at the time this test was given these special grades were, by virtue of the work they had done and were doing, really at the beginning of the 6th and 7th grades, respectively, their class scores are a year ahead of the standards set for the test.

The other way in which Scale Alpha 2 was scored was by multiplying the number of correct answers at each step of the scale by the value of the step and taking the sum of the products thus obtained. Table XXVI (on opposite page) displays the results by this method of scoring.

The difference in favor of the special room over the control rooms is much more marked with Scale Alpha 2 than with Scale A. It will be noticed that on the latter scale, the selected 5th grade in median score again excels the total 6th grade. This did not happen with the scores for Scale A, but it must be remembered that, as that scale was given, the control rooms had an advantage of three months' time over the experimental room—a circumstance which would tend to decrease somewhat the difference between them.

Summary

This chapter has been devoted to a consideration of the results obtained by applying various tests of ability in the fundamental branches of the course of study to the pupils of the experimental room at different times throughout the year. In some cases it has been possible to compare these results with standard scores or norms already evaluated or proposed. In other cases, the scores obtained in the experimental room have been compared with results secured by giving the same tests to a control group, made up of children in other rooms enrolling pupils of the same grades. Quality of handwriting was measured by the Ayres and Thorndike scales, spelling ability by Ayres' scale and Starch's lists, ability in the fundamental operations of arithmetic by the Woody arithmetic scales and the Woody-McCall scales in the mixed fundamentals, arithmetical reasoning by Bonser's tests for mathematical judgment, quality of composition by the Hillegas-Thorndike scale, linguistic ability of a more general type by

Trabue's completion-test language scales, ability to comprehend words by Thorndike's reading scale A, and ability to comprehend sentences by the same author's reading scale Alpha 2.

The results of these tests have been markedly consistent. When the pupils of the special room are measured by the scales and tests in any subject for which norms have been provided, they are found to be at least one year advanced. In every case, save two, when the scores of a test in the special room have been compared with the scores made by the control groups in the same test, it has been seen that the median score attained by the special 5th grade has reached or exceeded that made by the whole 6th grade of the school, treated as a single group, and including, it is to be remembered, the 6th-grade pupils enrolled in the special room. The two exceptions are found in the Woody-McCall Scale B I, when scored by time required for one correct solution (Table XVII) and in the Thorndike visual vocabulary reading scale, when scored by accuracy divided by time (Table XXV).

In the last chapter it was shown that, judged by the ordinary estimates of the quality of school work—teachers' marks, examination marks, and the like—the 5th-grade class of the experimental room had, by about the middle of the year, been recognized as ready and fit to go on with the work of the next grade, and that they had accordingly taken up that work. The same thing is true of the special 6th grade. The results of the tests which have been discussed in this chapter show that the 5th grade at that time had become in all reality a 6th grade—and not merely a 6th grade because it was doing the work of the 6th year in the course of study; it had been measured against the total 6th-grade group of the school, and had been found to equal or surpass it in median and average achievement. It has not been possible to measure the special 6th grade against the 7th grade of the school, but so far as we have been able to determine by the use of the tests for which standards are given, it, too, has justified the action of those in charge of it in allowing it to take up the work of the 7th grade. So long as only teachers' marks or opinions are offered as evidence in favor of the rapid advancement of bright pupils, the question may arise whether these pupils are advanced in anything more than name. In this particular case, however, the judgment of the teacher and the superintendent concerning the ability of the pupils to do the work of the next higher grade was corroborated by the more scientific scales and tests, which showed that, although these pupils were by May 1st a year ahead of where they would have been in the course of study had they remained in the regular rooms, they were not misplaced, at least so far as ability in the fundamental branches was concerned.

If we admit the validity of the various tests and scales, and if we admit that the conditions under which the experiment was carried out may be regarded as typical—and it is difficult to find any reason for not admitting it—then we have shown that children representing at least the top tenth of the 5th and 6th grades are able to do two years of the work of those grades in one year.

CHAPTER V

RESULTS OF A PRACTICE-TEST IN MULTIPLICATION

In order to secure information concerning the effects of practice, or drill, a practice-test in multiplication was carried on during the two weeks between February 23 and March 12, 1917. The material used for this experiment consisted of Sheets 15 and 16 of Thompson's *Minimum Essentials in Arithmetic.*[1] Sheet 16 is a quick-written test sheet in multiplication including products up to 100 not given in multiplication tables 1–12. It contains 162 indicated multiplications, each followed by a space in which the product is to be written, thus: 13×5= , 2×13= , and so on. Sheet 15 is a practice sheet of exactly similar character, save that it is printed on both sides, so that the incomplete multiplications on Side A are repeated on Side B, but in a different order.

On Friday, February 23, Sheet 16 was used in giving a check test to all the rooms in the building enrolling pupils in the 5th or 6th grades, namely, Room 5 Y, containing 38 pupils; Room 5–6 F, with 19 5th-grade and 19 6th-grade pupils; Room 6 G, enrolling 43 pupils in the 6th grade; and the 'experimental,' or 'special,' room, which at the time this test was given had a membership of 16 in the 5th and 16 in the 6th gràde (at about the middle of the year a pupil had been transferred to each of these grades from one of the regular rooms). It will be remembered that Rooms 5 Y, 5–6 F, and 6 G constitute what in previous chapters has been referred to as the "control group." The practice test itself was not carried out in Room 5-6 F, but that room was tested at the beginning and at the end of the experiment, and thus served as a check upon the improvement in the other rooms, the better so because it contained pupils of both the grades which were receiving practice.

[1] Ginn and Company, Publishers.

Method of Giving the Tests

In giving this initial test, the papers were distributed face down, the nature of the work to be done was carefully explained to the children, and they were told to work as rapidly as possible. At a given signal they turned the papers over and began work. As soon as any child had finished, he raised his hand, and his time, taken on a stop-watch, was immediately recorded. In scoring the papers, the per cent of accuracy was computed for each, and the time reduced to seconds. These two measures were combined into a single measure by dividing the time by the per cent of accuracy, thus obtaining a quantity which may be described as the number of seconds required to attain one per cent of accuracy. The same test was given at the close of the two weeks' practice and scored in the same way. The results of these two tests are exhibited in tables which will be included in the present chapter.

The actual practice was done under a somewhat different method. For this, Sheet 15, which has already been described, was used. Since this sheet is printed upon both sides, it was decided, in order to restrict the learning to the "multiplication facts" (to use Thompson's phrase) that are involved, to begin the practice on one side of the sheet one day and the other the next. Consequently, the first day's practice began on Side A, the second on Side B, and so on as long as the practice lasted. In this way, there was less opportunity for forming connections between adjacent products or for learning the products as a series down a column. In giving the practice tests the papers were distributed with the side upon which the day's practice was to begin turned down. Practically the same instructions and methods of beginning the work were used as in connection with the initial check test. Each day's practice was limited to ten minutes, at the end of which time a signal to stop was given, and the papers were collected. If any pupil succeeded in finishing the first side of the sheet before the end of the practice period, he turned the sheet over and began work on the other side. The few pupils who now and then succeeded in finishing both sides within the allotted ten minutes were at once supplied with another copy of the same sheet, handed them in such a way that they began work on the same side with which they had begun the first sheet.

The first practice test was given on Monday, February 27; the last one on Friday, March 9, with the final check test on the following Monday. It will be observed that Saturday and Sunday intervened between the initial test and the first practice, and that the same interruption came between the fifth and sixth practice periods, and between the last practice period and the final check test. All the tests were given at the same time of day in each room, and as nearly as possible at the same time in all the rooms. In Rooms 6G and 5Y they were given at 1:30 P.M., and in the special room at 2:00 P.M.[2] In Room 5-6F the check tests, which were the only ones given, were in each case given at three o'clock in the afternoon.

Method of Scoring

In scoring the results the pupils exchanged papers and marked mistakes as the correct products were read to them. The scoring of the pupils was afterwards checked, but almost no errors were found. The score for each paper was taken simply as the number of correct products written in ten minutes.

At the close of each day's practice the pupils were told their scores of the day before. These they recorded, and were thereby enabled to keep track of their progress. The effect of this was to ward off a drop in efficiency through loss of interest. Those who had the experiment in charge feel that there was no such loss, although at the close of the second week of practice there were signs that a decline in interest might have appeared, in the case of at least some of the pupils, had the experiment been continued much longer.

The accompanying tables show, by rooms and individuals, the daily scores (correct multiplications) made during the ten practice periods. No broken records are included; that is, the scores are given only for those pupils who were present for practice every day during the two weeks.

[2] The tests were given in Room 6G by the author, in the other rooms by Miss Coy.

TABLE XXVII

Improvement in Multiplication. Twenty-seven Fifth-Grade Pupils. Score by Number Correct Products. Room 5 Y

No.*	Mon.	Tues.	Wed.	Thur.	Fri.	Mon.	Tues.	Wed.	Thur.	Fri.
1........	98	113	105	117	130	129	129	141	157	156
2........	201	213	239	240	270	267	292	278	298	290
3........	69	84	68	99	88	105	108	110	113	121
5........	187	182	188	183	202	160	254	236	251	272
6........	63	65	60	75	88	71	79	106	104	131
10........	53	66	60	72	79	82	88	82	108	120
11........	120	132	159	178	196	175	189	204	202	184
12........	57	86	64	106	111	115	133	122	123	142
13........	84	83	67	53	84	87	88	94	95	96
14........	98	96	96	113	113	113	141	144	150	161
16........	199	180	196	185	205	202	223	203	187	203
17........	131	135	158	162	154	136	166	160	173	175
18........	111	119	135	153	165	163	178	186	188	195
19........	137	117	118	153	158	161	167	178	193	213
20........	91	82	79	108	117	103	143	130	129	147
21........	97	100	111	131	141	158	161	161	176	175
22........	58	56	53	55	85	94	91	107	110	146
23........	168	157	146	170	159	166	184	197	222	218
24........	71	94	111	120	137	125	150	157	144	145
26........	108	114	130	140	150	147	174	170	176	181
27........	67	76	77	71	75	94	93	84	95	103
28........	130	149	154	173	183	169	196	197	210	212
29........	88	90	110	143	147	149	168	162	174	172
30........	93	88	103	100	123	127	135	149	155	180
32........	79	74	96	77	95	102	122	170	135	129
37........	79	78	90	101	113	123	116	134	156	150
41........	88	92	95	114	120	132	149	147	133	137
Average...	100.96	108.2	113.6	125.8	136.6	135.4	153.2	155.9	161.4	172.4

* Breaks in numbering are caused by the omission of incomplete records.

TABLE XXVIII

Improvement in Multiplication. Twenty-nine Sixth-Grade Pupils. Score by Number Correct Products. Room 6 G

No.	Mon.	Tues.	Wed.	Thur.	Fri.	Mon.	Tues.	Wed.	Thur.	Fri.
1........	209	247	266	311	315	349	354	390	375	345
2........	152	168	181	194	195	181	214	237	235	205
3........	140	151	170	189	198	193	189	202	212	215
4........	169	168	184	172	235	224	242	275	281	271
5........	216	243	285	299	352	365	375	398	387	391
6........	106	99	112	128	140	146	144	166	175	184
7........	174	198	211	255	266	275	295	314	306	304
9........	114	122	128	131	132	147	162	163	149	167
10........	69	93	113	110	125	117	132	156	158	165
11........	165	180	183	209	230	248	232	239	245	275
12........	67	85	113	107	130	124	142	152	138	140
13........	147	166	179	203	216	236	230	246	238	243
14........	110	121	127	149	139	151	169	174	167	177
15........	193	221	238	289	266	257	232	290	267	277
16........	60	65	68	77	99	118	110	127	120	125
18........	118	149	140	179	161	179	190	190	193	203
20........	182	194	218	250	254	253	268	292	316	345
21........	53	78	94	117	109	101	128	121	115	127
23........	195	208	199	223	218	228	229	252	231	212
24........	120	128	135	122	123	136	173	165	176	186
25........	157	166	199	190	186	212	218	230	243	267
28........	95	106	125	133	126	119	128	156	160	164
29........	185	239	209	242	246	286	314	343	306	345
30........	56	102	95	119	118	111	156	174	157	187
32........	71	73	78	83	90	94	95	89	99	113
37........	135	148	117	167	187	193	199	193	178	200
39........	204	252	251	286	297	314	230	333	330	331
40........	80	65	96	98	123	117	136	140	144	145
43........	47	64	52	70	64	84	72	72	88	129
Average...	130.7	148.3	157.5	175.8	184.1	188.6	202.0	216.5	213.1	222.0

TABLE XXIX

Improvement in Multiplication. Special Room

Grade	No.	Mon.	Tues.	Wed.	Thur.	Fri.	Mon.	Tues.	Wed.	Thur.	Fri.
	1	90	92	128	116	153	147	153	168	187	194
	2	115	98	132	142	174	153	149	124	152	168
	3	122	161	175	189	203	194	201	214	211	226
	4	73	76	96	94	124	129	135	137	154	194
	5	78	100	118	146	159	160	163	159	186	175
	6	99	99	81	114	130	131	146	151	158	165
V	8	118	99	118	140	137	150	155	175	185	193
	10	126	156	168	186	192	193	194	204	198	205
	11	111	145	142	136	160	162	152	174	174	175
	13	134	105	108	116	104	135	151	134	157	164
	14	60	76	93	99	96	106	102	115	120	129
	15	104	113	152	151	174	150	161	187	204	211
	31	95	89	94	111	105	114	110	126	130	144
Average..		101.9	108.4	123.5	133.8	147.0	148.1	151.7	159.1	170.5	180.2
	16	130	144	156	166	160	163	169	175	185	184
	17	169	184	193	213	218	217	245	254	276	323
	18	221	223	220	270	278	301	301	319	358	383
	19	174	188	233	257	256	222	246	277	275	300
	20	160	193	199	215	222	225	242	275	228	258
	21	153	142	142	170	157	152	150	186	202	209
	22	116	98	145	160	150	148	170	176	176	167
VI	23	98	126	146	151	156	158	155	169	192	177
	24	158	160	190	189	209	205	232	234	257	277
	25	171	184	193	210	216	222	218	242	246	267
	26	185	198	232	213	240	233	231	271	298	331
	27	247	298	356	264	365	379	370	402	393	405
	28	139	165	184	222	239	243	243	247	264	269
	29	186	195	200	208	214	242	264	275	293	279
	30	160	162	179	198	206	215	231	221	224	256
	32	100	92	123	119	137	155	177	174	181	198
Average..		160.4	172.0	193.2	207.8	213.9	217.5	227.8	243.6	253.0	267.7

The Practice-Curves

These tables and the curves drawn from them are sufficiently self-evident as to need little discussion. Just a few features may be pointed out, however. In the first place, it will be noticed that on the first day of the practice test, the average ability of the 5th-grade control group and the special 5th-grade group was practically the same (about 101 correct solutions in the ten minutes of practice time). At the end of the ten periods of practice, the average score of the control group was 172, while that of the special group was 180. Of course, this is not a great difference even yet, but it must be remembered that a difference of eight correct solutions at that level represents a larger difference in attainment than a difference of eight solutions at the level at which the test began. The difference is more marked in the case of the 6th-grade groups. The control group began with an average score of 131 and made a gross gain of 91, while the selected group began 30 multiplications above them and made a gross gain of 107, so that the difference between the two groups, in average score, was larger at the close of the practice than at the beginning, and the difference is all the greater when we take into consideration the increased difficulty attending improvement as the upper limit is more and more closely approached.

Inspection of the curves drawn from the daily averages of the several groups reveals a check in their rise, located at the sixth period, which came on a Monday. In this, the influence of the lack of practice on Saturday and Sunday may be shown. It will also be observed that this loss was rather quickly made up. In only two instances did any group in its average score fall below a score which it had already attained, and only one of these is of any consequence. This happened in Room 6G, or the 6th-grade control group, just after the middle of the second week. It is the opinion of the writer that the great increase in the room's score upon Wednesday of that week was due to an increased enthusiasm arising from a general agreement among the pupils that they would see how good a record they could make. If such was the case, there was a slight falling off in enthusiasm next day, although Friday's score in turn exceeded the high score made on Wednesday. It is difficult to determine in any such experiment just what part is played by changes in the attitude of the subjects (rivalry, increase and decrease of interest, ideals of accuracy, etc.). It really does not matter so much, however, since these things are characteristic traits which enter quite intimately into the work of learning, so that to try to eliminate them from a practice experiment like this would create an artificial situation. Since the aim of the experiment was to see how much improvement these children could make in learning these particular number combinations under actual school conditions, it was considered unwise to caution them against doing things which they otherwise might not think of, and for that reason nothing was said about practice at home or elsewhere outside of the of the time set apart for it in the schoolroom. So far as could be learned after the experiment was finished, very little, if any, outside practice was engaged in.

Results of the Check Tests

To secure data concerning improvement in speed and accuracy, as well as to obtain a check upon the experiment in general, the test which has been described above as the initial and final check test was given to all the rooms which took part in the practice, as well as to another room containing pupils of the same grades, but which did not participate in the practice series proper. Tables XXX to XXXIII, inclusive, show the results obtained by these tests. In interpreting the figures given in the last two columns of each of these tables, namely, the quotients obtained by dividing the time by the accuracy, it must be remembered that the smaller the figure, the higher the degree of attainment.

TABLE XXX

Results of Initial and Final Check Tests. Fifth-Grade Pupils. Room 5 Y

Pupil's Number	Per Cent. of Accuracy		Time in Seconds		Time ÷ Accuracy	
	Initial	Final	Initial	Final	Initial	Final
1	96.9	98.1	802	640	8.3	6.5
2	98.1	99.4	583	327	5.9	3.3
3	99.4	98.1	1183	849	11.9	8.7
5	99.4	93.8	660	364	6.7	3.9
6	97.5	97.5	1170	892	12.0	9.2
10	98.8	99.4	1350	888	13.7	8.9
11	99.4	99.4	870	458	8.8	4.6
13	79.0	83.3	1170	814	14.8	9.8
14	94.4	96.3	836	606	8.8	6.3
16	100.0	100.0	505	445	5.0	4.5
17	99.4	99.4	690	597	7.0	6.0
18	95.1	96.9	1710	616	18.0	6.4
19	98.8	98.1	1000	474	10.1	4.8
20	93.8	97.5	805	652	8.6	5.7
21	100.0	98.1	1020	558	10.2	5.7
22	91.9	96.3	1235	944	13.4	9.8
23	99.4	99.4	705	447	7.1	4.5
24	96.3	98.1	1030	740	10.7	7.6
26	100.0	100.0	1590	570	15.9	5.7
27	97.5	99.4	1125	825	11.5	8.3
28	100.0	99.4	775	465	7.7	4.7
29	98.8	98.1	900	486	9.1	4.9
32	96.9	96.9	1155	816	11.9	8.4
37	98.8	98.1	1035	647	10.5	6.67
41	95.1	94.4	1070	750	11.3	7.9
Average	97.0	97.4	959	608	10.4	6.5
Poorest	79.0	83.3	1710	944	18.0	9.8
Best	100.0	100.0	505	327	5.0	3.3

TABLE XXXI

Results of Initial and Final Check Tests. Sixth-Grade Pupils. Room 6 G

No.	PER CENT. OF ACCURACY		TIME IN SECONDS		TIME ÷ ACCURACY	
	Initial	Final	Initial	Final	Initial	Final
1	96.9	95.1	520	315	5.4	3.3
2	99.4	98.8	771	429	7.8	4.3
3	96.9	99.4	545	505	5.6	5.1
4	96.9	95.7	480	328	5.0	3.5
5	98.1	93.2	780	245	8.0	2.6
6	96.9	98.8	552	605	5.7	6.1
7	98.8	79.0	605	300	6.1	3.8
9	100.0	97.5	1050	625	10.5	6.4
10	98.8	100.0	780	630	7.9	6.3
11	96.3	95.1	561	405	5.8	4.3
12	98.8	94.4	830	570	8.4	6.0
13	98.8	99.4	630	400	6.4	4.0
15	95.1	96.9	562	404	5.9	4.2
16	96.3	100.0	940	835	9.9	8.4
18	98.1	95.1	610	470	6.2	4.9
20	98.8	99.4	548	315	5.6	3.2
21	98.8	100.0	830	875	8.4	8.8
23	96.3	96.9	450	364	4.7	3.8
24	98.8	95.1	725	545	7.3	5.7
25	93.8	77.7	600	260	6.4	3.4
28	97.5	95.1	840	745	8.6	7.8
29	99.4	99.4	560	420	5.6	4.2
30	87.1	96.9	1390	605	16.0	6.2
32	95.7	100.0	950	775	10.0	7.8
37	95.7	92.6	770	526	8.0	5.7
39	100.0	98.1	490	280	4.9	2.9
40	96.3	100.0	720	655	7.5	6.6
43	99.4	99.4	1500	955	15.1	9.6
Average	93.9	96.0	744	527.7	7.33	5.3
Poorest	87.1	77.7	1500	955.0	15.1	9.6
Best	100.0	100.0	450	260.0	4.5	2.6

TABLE XXXII

Results of Initial and Final Check Tests. Special Room

Grade	No.	PER CENT OF ACCURACY		TIME IN SECONDS		TIME ÷ ACCURACY	
		Initial	Final	Initial	Final	Initial	Final
V	1	99.4	98.8	1042	450	10.5	4.6
	2	96.9	99.4	825	510	8.5	5.1
	3	96.3	95.7	703	305	7.3	3.2
	4	99.4	100.0	1341	792	13.8	7.9
	5	99.4	99.4	1170	556	11.8	5.6
	6	95.7	99.4	1178	623	12.3	6.3
	8	99.4	99.4	805	432	8.1	4.4
	10	98.8	99.4	760	406	7.7	4.1
	11	97.6	98.1	883	504	9.1	5.1
	13	98.8	97.5	1053	526	10.7	5.4
	14	100.0	100.0	1232	712	12.3	7.1
	15	99.4	98.8	1070	495	10.8	5.0
	31	100.0	99.4	830	600	8.3	6.0
Average	......	98.5	98.9	999	531	10.1	5.3
Poorest	......	95.7	95.7	1341	792	13.5	7.9
Best	......	100.0	100.0	703	305	7.3	3.2
VI	16	96.9	96.9	863	380	8.9	3.9
	17	98.8	99.4	703	317	7.1	3.2
	18	99.4	96.9	457	227	4.6	2.3
	19	98.8	98.1	616	304	6.2	3.1
	20	99.4	99.4	590	390	6.0	3.9
	21	95.1	96.3	827	460	8.7	4.8
	22	98.1	98.1	765	535	7.8	5.5
	23	97.5	96.9	856	485	8.3	5.0
	24	95.1	95.7	710	317	7.5	3.3
	25	98.8	98.8	780	328	7.9	3.3
	26	98.8	98.1	540	225	5.5	2.3
	27	96.9	99.4	410	215	4.2	2.1
	28	98.8	97.5	621	325	6.3	3.3
	29	97.5	94.4	612	290	6.3	3.1
	30	99.4	98.8	685	335	6.9	3.4
	32	99.4	100.0	930	548	9.4	5.5
Average	......	98.0	97.8	685	355	7.01	3.6
Poorest	......	95.1	94.4	930	548	8.9	5.5
Best	......	100.0	100.0	410	215	4.2	2.1

TABLE XXXIII

Results of Initial and Final Check Tests. Room 5-6 F (Unpracticed Room)

		PER CENT. OF ACCURACY		TIME IN SECONDS		TIME ÷ ACCURACY	
Grade	No.	Initial	Final	Initial	Final	Initial	Final
	1	96.9	98.1	945	807	9.8	8.2
	2	93.2	98.1	740	642	7.9	6.5
	3	100.0	99.4	1003	912	10.0	9.2
	4	98.8	95.7	1144	827	11.6	8.6
	5	91.3	95.7	1183	1120	13.0	11.7
	6	97.5	97.5	952	960	9.8	9.9
V..........	7	96.3	96.3	1190	1118	12.4	11.6
	8	98.1	99.4	772	683	8.9	6.9
	9	96.9	99.4	1250	1273	12.9	12.8
	10	96.9	95.7	820	805	8.5	8.4
	11	96.3	100.0	825	875	8.6	8.8
	12	99.4	96.3	845	687	8.5	7.2
	13	96.9	96.9	1006	912	10.4	9.4
	14	98.1	95.7	1054	933	10.8	9.8
Average	......	96.9	97.4	989	897	10.2	9.2
Poorest.	......	91.3	95.7	1250	1273	13.0	12.8
Best....	......	100.0	100.0	740	642	7.9	6.5
	15	100.0	98.8	706	642	7.1	6.5
	16	99.4	98.1	875	703	8.8	7.8
	17	99.4	99.4	505	475	5.1	4.8
	18	100.0	100.0	805	623	8.8	6.2
	19	95.7	93.8	937	834	9.8	8.9
	20	100.0	99.4	1125	742	11.2	7.5
VI.........	21	98.8	87.7	1332	1110	13.5	12.7
	22	95.1	98.8	1026	877	10.8	8.9
	23	96.3	96.9	695	820	7.2	8.5
	24	98.1	95.1	660	496	6.7	5.2
	25	97.5	99.4	828	706	8.5	7.1
	26	98.1	98.8	1200	875	9.4	8.9
	27	98.1	98.8	440	380	4.5	3.9
Average	......	98.2	97.3	835	714	8.51	7.4
Poorest.	......	93.2	93.8	1332	1110	13.5	12.7
Best....	......	100.0	100.0	440	380	4.5	3.9

Nature of the Improvement

The improvement has been, of course, an improvement in speed, because the accuracy was already close to the upper limit at the beginning of practice. Many of the number combinations called for were already known, and the rest could readily be computed mentally, so that any inaccuracy here implies carelessness rather than lack of knowledge. The activities demanded were not wholly mental, for in addition to the computation of the required result, in case it was not known, there was demanded the physical act of writing it down. Improvement in time, therefore, might take place along at least two lines; (1) a product once learned might be written at once, without the loss of time in calculation, and (2) there might be a gain of speed in writing the results upon the practice sheet. It is obvious that the larger amount of gain resulted from improvement in the first direction, though there were instances of a marked saving in time through the development of a more expeditious method of writing the results, as, for instance, that of writing the two-place products in the regular order of the tens' digit first, instead of writing the unit figure before the tens' figure. This change generally took place when the product had been learned so that the calculation of it was no longer necessary. Of the different practice groups, the 5th-grade class in the special room had the highest average per cent of accuracy at the beginning of the experiment, and retained it until the close. The special 6th-grade made no gain in this respect, but suffered a slight loss. This class, however, when measured by the single score of time divided by accuracy, shows by far the greatest improvement, owing to its remarkable increase in speed. It is worth noting that in this test, as in the great majority of the educational tests discussed in the preceding chapter, the average score (in time divided by accuracy) of the special 5th grade reaches that attained by the 6th-grade pupils of the control group, though considerably lower at the beginning. *Two weeks' drill, therefore, has brought this special 5th-grade group, which at the time of the experiment had done about six weeks of 6th-grade work, up to the level of a class which had been doing the regular 6th-grade work for seven months.*

By comparing the gains made in the practiced groups with those made by children of the same grades in the unpracticed room, the results of the drill are readily made apparent. It is interesting to note, in this connection, that the unpracticed room actually does show a respectable gain. This may be due to several factors. In the first place, learning occurred in connection with the first application of the test and some of the combinations learned were remembered. Again, familiarity with the method of the test had been acquired, which would result in a saving of time. In addition to these, the regular work of the schoolroom in arithmetic had afforded incidental practice in multiplication, and the two weeks of training might well have functioned in the results of the final test.

Practice and Individual Differences

A study of the individual learning curves obtained in this multiplication drill, as well as of the curves showing the daily room averages confirms the conclusion, laid down by so many investigators, that practice, so far from equalizing individual differences, tends to increase them. To the pupil with high initial ability, in the great majority of our cases, this drill has given opportunity to reach an even higher degree of superiority. Not much change of rank has taken place. In general, those who led at the initial test also led in the final. If the two grades of the special room are treated as one group, it will be seen that the highest three individuals in the initial test occupy their respective positions in the final test, with no change of rank at all. The correlation between pupils' ranks in the two tests, for the special room, figured by the "foot-rule" method is .63, which by the conversion table gives us a Pearson correlation of $r = .84$.[3]

Our results then, to repeat what has been said above, are in complete accord with those of other investigators who have found high initial ability no barrier to profit by training, and practice in any given performance more efficient in case of those with high initial ability in the desired performance, granted only that the high initial ability does not represent a close approach to the upper limit already obtained by previous practice. To quote from Wells:

> ". . . A superior performance at the beginning of special practice is not necessarily, or even probably, attained at the sacrifice of prospects for further improvement. A high initial efficiency may carry with it as much or more prospect of improvement under special practice than a low one. It was not because the favored individual had had more of the general experience enabling him to meet the experimental situation better, but because he possessed the native ability to profit more by such experience, general and special, past and future. Not practice, but *practiceability*, is responsible for the superior position of such an individual; and, in broader aspect, not education, but educability.[4]

[3] For process of calculating correlation by the "foot-rule" method, and for conversion table, see Whipple's *Manual*, Part I, pp. 42–44.

[4] Wells, F. L. The relation of practice to individual differences. *American Journal of Psychology*, 23:75–88.

Also see, Thorndike, E. L. The effect of practice in the case of a purely intellectual function. *American Journal of Psychology*, 18:374–384.

Donovan, M. E. and Thorndike, E. L. Improvement in a practice experiment under school conditions. *American Journal of Psychology*, 24:426–428.

For a complete treatment of the learning-curve, see Thorndike, E. L. *Educational Psychology*, Volume II, *The Psychology of Learning*; and for the effect of practice upon individual differences see Volume III of the same work, *Work and Fatigue and Individual Differences*.

CHAPTER VI

RESULTS OF THE MENTAL TESTS

In this chapter will be discussed the results of a few of the tests[1] which were given to the pupils of the special room, as well as to those in the control groups. The tests treated here are more general in their nature than those which were described in Chapter IV, and, being psychological rather than educational, they show primarily differences in native ability, rather than in ability which has been developed by training in some special line.

LOGICAL MEMORY

Whipple's "*Marble Statue* test"[2] is a test for 'logical,' or 'substance' memory, or what is known as 'memory for ideas.' A simple version of the story of Pygmalion and Galatea is read to the subject, who has previously been warned to give close attention in order that he may be able to reproduce what he hears. The test is scored on the basis of the number of ideas satisfactorily reproduced, rather than upon an exact, verbatim reproduction of the passage as presented. The story is made up of 67 standard divisions, each one of which constitutes an 'idea.' The reproduction is scored by comparing it with the standard idea-divisions of the original passage. Table XXXIV shows the results of this test. Reproduction was begun immediately after the passage had been read, and the score is expressed as the number of ideas satisfactorily reproduced.

This test was given in the experimental room on October 26, and in the other rooms on January 24, or three months later. Notwithstanding this handicap in time, the superiority of the selected group is clearly evident. As was the case in the majority of the educational tests, the 5th-grade class of the special room, in median score, exceeds the total group of 6th-grade pupils.

[1] For a fuller account of the mental tests, see G. M. Whipple, *Classes for Gifted Children*, 1919.

[2] *Manual of Mental and Physical Tests*, Pt. II.

TABLE XXXIV

Marble Statue Test. Immediate Reproduction. Number of Ideas Reproduced

Score	NUMBER OF PUPILS					
	Fifth Grade			Sixth Grade		
	Total	Control	Selected	Total	Control	Selected
17–18	.....	3	0	.....	1	0
19–20	.....	0	0	.....	1	0
21–22	.....	4	0	.....	3	0
23–24	.....	5	0	.....	6	0
25–26	.....	5	0	.....	2	0
27–28	.....	8	1	.....	8	0
29–30	.....	6	4	.....	4	1
31–32	.....	1	0	.....	9	2
33–34	.....	4	2	.....	7	2
35–36	.....	4	2	.....	7	0
37–38	.....	4	2	.....	2	1
39–40	.....	2	2	.....	6	3
41–42	.....	2	0	.....	1	4
43–44	.....	0	1	.....	0	1
45–46	.....	1	0	.....	2	0
47–48	.....	0	1	.....	0	0
49–50	.....	0	0	.....	0	0
51–52	.....	0	0	.....	1	1
Sum	.....	49	15	.....	60	15
Group:						
Median	30.30	28.75	35.50	33.10	31.50	40.30
Average	30.79	29.39	35.40	32.98	31.59	38.53
Range	17–48	17–42	27–48	18–51	18–51	30–51

Bonser's Reasoning Tests

In order to compare ability in certain forms of reasoning, more particularly selective judgment, Bonser's Tests III, V, and VI were used. Those parts of Test III which were given consist of two sets of ten sentences each, with a significant word omitted from each to be filled in by the pupil; and two sets of ten sentences in each of which are placed, one above the other, two significant words, one of which would give an erroneous meaning to the sentence and is to be crossed out by the pupil so as to make the sentence read correctly (Test III, Aa, Ab, Ba and Bb). Bonser says that this test involves recognition and selection on the basis of fitness to purpose as the dominant factor, and that the activity tested is that of accuracy and spontaneity in recognizing resemblances between the known of experience and the unknown of new situations. Test V, A and B, consists of two series each of ten reasons why some given statement is true. Some of these reasons are correct, others irrelevant or incorrect, and the pupil is to select the correct ones. Test VI contains two sets, of three series each of definitions for a given thing or term (some correct, others incorrect or irrelevant) from among which the pupil is to select those that are correct. In giving these tests, as well as in scoring them, Bonser's directions were observed precisely.[3] The tests were given first in the special room, and the time-limit for each of the tests in the other rooms was fixed at the number of seconds which it took the first pupil in the special room to finish that test. The following table shows the amalgamated scores for all three of the tests, *i.e.*, the scores made by each pupil in the different tests, combined into a single score by adding.

TABLE XXXV

Bonser's Reasoning Tests; III, V, and VI. Combined Scores

Score	NUMBER OF PUPILS					
	Fifth Grade			Sixth Grade		
	Total	Control	Selected	Total	Control	Selected
1– 5	.....	1	0	.....	0	0
6–10	.....	2	0	.....	0	0
11–15	.....	5	0	.....	1	0
16–20	.....	6	0	.....	4	0
21–25	.....	2	0	.....	11	0
26–30	.....	7	1	.....	4	0
31–35	.....	4	3	.....	2	3
36–40	.....	4	3	.....	5	0
41–45	.....	3	2	.....	8	1
46–50	.....	2	1	.....	4	0
51–55	.....	3	2	.....	4	4
56–60	.....	2	0	.....	5	1
61–65	.....	2	1	.....	2	2
66–70	.....	1	1	.....	0	0
71–75	.....	0	0	.....	0	0
76–80	.....	0	1	.....	2	2
81–85	.....	0	0	.....	0	1
86–90	.....	0	0	.....	1	0
91–95	.....	1	0	.....	0	1
Sum	.....	45	15	.....	53	15
Group:						
Median	35.64	30.30	43.50	43.50	40.00	55.00
Average	36.64	33.46	46.17	40.28	35.02	58.86
Range	5–91	5–91	27–76.5	13–95	13–86	31.5–95

[3] Bonser, F. G. *The Reasoning Ability of Children of the Fourth, Fifth, and Sixth School Grades.* Teachers College, Columbia University Contributions to Education, No. 37, pp. 3–18.

These tests were given in the special room on the 5th, 6th, and 7th of December, and in the regular rooms a month later. According to the results, the pupils of the special room were distinctly superior to the others in selective judgment, and it is once more the case that the special 5th grade excelled the score of the whole 6th-grade group.

Equivalent Proverbs

Another of the tests used was the "Equivalent Proverbs Test." This test was given in three parts, each consisting of a series of well-known English proverbs and a series of African or Arabian proverbs,

TABLE XXXVI

Equivalent Proverbs Test. Combined Scores

Score	NUMBER OF PUPILS					
	Fifth Grade			Sixth Grade		
	Total	Control	Selected	Total	Control	Selected
580–599	.....	0	0	.....	1	0
560–579	.....	0	0	.....	1	0
420–559	.....	0	0	.....	0	0
400–419	.....	1	0	.....	0	0
380–399	.....	1	0	.....	1	0
360–379	.....	0	0	.....	0	0
340–359	.....	3	0	.....	0	0
320–339	.....	0	0	.....	0	0
300–319	.....	0	0	.....	1	0
280–299	.....	2	0	.....	2	0
260–279	.....	0	0	.....	1	0
240–259	.....	3	0	.....	2	0
220–239	.....	2	0	.....	0	0
200–219	.....	3	0	.....	1	0
180–199	.....	5	1	.....	4	0
160–179	.....	1	1	.....	1	2
140–159	.....	5	3	.....	6	1
120–139	.....	7	3	.....	5	1
100–119	.....	2	2	.....	11	1
80– 99	.....	2	0	.....	8	0
60– 79	.....	8	2	.....	3	7
40– 59	.....	0	2	.....	3	3
20– 39	.....	0	0	.....	2	0
Sum	.....	45	14	.....	52	15
Group:						
Median	145.0	156.0	132.4	115.0	118.60	72.9
Average	163.4	177.8	117.0	135.6	148.75	90.0
Range	419–40.5	419–60	190.2-40.5	576–39.6	576–39.6	177–41.7

arranged in parallel columns. The task was to find for each English proverb the equivalent proverb in the other list. In some respects this test is similar to Bonser's reasoning tests, in that it may be said to test ability in seeing relationships in verbal expressions. Each of the three parts was given separately to all the rooms at practically the same time, and was scored by dividing the time in seconds required to finish it by the number of correct identifications. The three scores for each pupil in this manner were then added, to afford a single final score. Since each score by this method represents the time required for one correct solution, it will be remembered that the higher figures represent the lower scores.

Because of the wide range over which these scores are scattered, and the irregularity of their distribution, there is for each grade a considerable difference between the median and the average. Each of the special grades, however, shows marked superiority over its control group, and the difference seems somewhat greater in case of the 6th grade. In that grade, however, two individuals in the control group succeeded in making better scores than were made in the selected group.

Word-Building

Whipple's "Word-building Test"[4] might have been considered among the language tests discussed in Chapter IV, for successful performance in this test is conditioned to some extent upon size and readiness of vocabulary. In addition, Whipple says that "it is one that calls for ingenuity and active attention; it might fairly be said to demand that ability to combine isolated fragments into a whole, which Ebbinghaus has declared to be the essence of intelligence and for the measurement of which he devised his well-known 'completion method.' " This test is given in two parts, by means of two blanks, one of which calls for the combining of words from the letters *a, e, o, b, m, t;* the other from the letters *e, a, i, r, l, p.* The *aeobmt* blank is given first, followed by the *eairlp* blank, and five minutes is allowed for each. The score of the individual's performance is the sum of the legitimate words formed from the two lists. This test was given to the experimental room on October 24, and to the other rooms about three months later.

[4] *Manual,* Part II, pp. 274–283.

TABLE XXXVII

Word-Building Test. Combined Scores of Both Lists

Score	Number of Pupils					
	Fifth Grade			Sixth Grade		
	Total	Control	Selected	Total	Control	Selected
2– 3	.....	1	0	.....	0	0
4– 5	.....	1	0	.....	0	0
6– 7	.....	0	0	.....	0	0
8– 9	.....	0	1	.....	2	0
10–11	.....	1	1	.....	0	1
12–13	.....	7	0	.....	2	1
14–15	.....	5	1	.....	7	0
16–17	.....	6	2	.....	5	0
18–19	.....	4	0	.....	7	2
20–21	.....	6	1	.....	7	0
22–23	.....	5	2	.....	3	1
24–25	.....	4	1	.....	10	2
26–27	.....	2	3	.....	2	4
28–29	.....	1	2	.....	6	1
30–31	.....	1	0	.....	3	0
32–33	.....	3	0	.....	1	1
34–35	.....	0	0	.....	1	1
36–37	.....	0	0	.....	0	1
Sum	.....	47	14	.....	56	15
Group:						
Median	20.29	18.62	22.5	22.40	21.57	26.50
Average	19.50	19.06	21.0	22.14	21.27	24.70
Range	2–33	2–33	9–29	9–37	9–34	10–37

With this test, as with the preceding one, the special 6th-grade class shows a somewhat larger difference in its favor than does the special 5th-grade. If we take into account the difference in time, it seems fair to say that the special 5th grade shows a median and an average score practically equal to that of the whole 6th grade; especially so since the percentile curves of word-building published by Whipple show that, at the age of these pupils, the growth for three months in ability in this test, as measured by the median score, is approximately one word. When this correction is applied to the median and average scores of the control groups, the superiority of the selected group is more clearly revealed. It is true, however, that four individuals in the 5th-grade control group made a higher score than was made by any member of the special class in the same grade.

Summary

The results of the tests described in this chapter go to show that bright children excel ordinary ones in such things as logical memory and selective judgment, as well as in performance in the school subjects, as was shown in Chapter IV. In other words, the differences between the top tenth of the children in the middle grades and the rest of the children in those grades, are differences which to a great extent depend upon heredity, rather than upon training. The same thing is indicated by the results of the practice test discussed in the preceding chapter, as well as by those of a great number of other mental tests which were given throughout the year, but which it has not been thought necessary to discuss, inasmuch as a complete description of them has been published elsewhere. The evidence of all the tests strongly suggests that the intellectual differences between bright and mediocre children are of such an amount that they practically may be considered qualitative as well. At any rate the results of the tests indicate that gifted children have mental powers which are sufficiently different from those of average children to make it probable that the pedagogy of gifted children must include a special adaptation of method to their peculiar needs. The nature of this adaptation will be made the subject of the next chapter.

CHAPTER VII

METHODS OF TEACHING AS ADAPTED TO THE INSTRUCTION OF GIFTED CHILDREN

While we have a few accounts of the operation of special classes for gifted children, almost nothing has been said concerning the special pedagogy of such classes. It would seem that this phase of the work has so far received but little attention in comparison with that which has been given to plans for organization, suggestions for programs of study, and discussions of the special aims to be attained by segregating the brighter pupils. Very much more, too, has been written about the results which have been obtained in such rooms than about the methods by which those results were secured. This chapter will be devoted to a discussion of such modifications of teaching-method as seem advisable in the conduct of a special room, or class, for children of better than normal ability. Its conclusions are based upon the results of plans which were definitely tried out in the experimental room, observation of three other special rooms for superior children, conferences with a few teachers of such rooms, and correspondence with supervising officers and teachers having such rooms in charge.

Of the few studies of this particular problem which are available, one grew out of the work of the special room established in Cincinnati in 1910,[1] and was reported by Miss Flora Unrich, who had the room in her care. Miss Unrich says in her article that soon after entering upon her work with these pupils she took an inventory of their mental equipments and characteristics, their strengths and their weaknesses, and concluded that the qualities which she needed to implant in them were self-control, self-helpfulness (adaptability), concentration, and continuity. She attempted, then, to develop self-helpfulness by doing nothing for a child which he could do for himself; and to develop accuracy, thoroughness, and continuity by

[1] See Chapter II.

not allowing her pupils to do anything in a desultory way, or to leave anything unfinished. For training in concentration she gave them practice in doing work while recitations were going on. In consequence of this treatment, as she says, her pupils developed in power to concentrate, to select (form judgments), and to examine themselves, as well as in will to finish what they had once begun. In order that these pupils might have no opportunity to form habits of indolence, whenever any assigned task had proved too easy they were at once provided with additional material difficult enough to enlist a deeper interest and call out greater efforts. Of the 32 pupils who were enrolled in this room, 25 accomplished two years of work during the year it was in session. This gain, says Miss Unrich, was made possible "by avoiding all mechanical teaching, appealing to the reason and judgment of the pupils, reducing all drill to a minimum, studying carefully in advance the entire year's course, and selecting kindred facts and subjects. This made much correlation possible, and prevented dissipation and side-tracking of the pupils' energies, by presenting such material when it could be effectively assimilated." Other features which were stressed are free and independent expression, power of initiative, careful self-censorship, conscientious effort, confidence placed in the pupils and understood by them to be met in only one way, individualization of instruction, and adjustment of the work to individual needs.[2]

An interesting article by Dr. Martha Adler describes an attempt to adapt methods of instruction to bright pupils which was made in Public School 77, New York City. The premise underlying the experiment was that "pupils of advanced intelligence should not only make more rapid progress than those of younger mental age, but that methods of instruction should be adapted to mental maturity." Seventy 1st-grade boys, about to begin the second half of the 1st-grade work, were tested by Goddard's 1911 Revision of the Binet Scale. The 35 boys who tested highest were placed in Class A, or the advanced section; and the others were assigned to Class B, the regular section. In describing the work of these two sections, Dr. Adler says:

[2] Unrich, Flora. A year's work in a "superior" class. *Psychological Clinic*, 5: January, 1912, 245–250.

"In each class progress was made at a rate commensurate with the abilities of the children. In Class A, particular supervision was given to the instruction in reading and in the writing of phonetic elements leading to spelling, the purpose being to replace, at an early stage, low-grade by high-grade habits. Audible lip-preparation of new reading-matter and pointing to the words with the fingers are usually permitted with young pupils. Silent reading, with eye-recognition of the words was substituted at an early stage. Rapid reading and thought-getting were secured by various devices, and a maturity in development was noted which is not customary with young pupils. The synthetic method of writing phonograms usually precedes the analytic resolution into the letter elements by a considerable period. In the present instance, it was possible to combine these methods at a much earlier time than is customary. In the work in arithmetic it was noted that a much shorter period was needed by the pupils for objective work, and it was not a difficult task for them to acquire the more advanced work."

In the same school, out of a class of eighty-nine 4th-grade boys were selected the 36 who made the best showing in a selected list of mental tests. These were placed in a special section and their teacher was told to advance at a rate commensurate with their abilities. Concerning the methods used in this advanced section, the author of the study says:

"In the advanced section special effort was made to engender the higher habits of independent study; the selection of the main thought of a paragraph or page, the organization of minor details around larger topics, and the cultivation of initiative in the use of a textbook and other aids to study were particularly emphasized. Combining the work of the latter half of the fourth grade with that of the first half of the fifth was successfully done by the teacher."[3]

A teacher in one of the 'preparatory centers' of Baltimore in speaking of the methods used in her classes and in the school in general, says that one of the chief aims is that the pupils develop habits of promptness and concentration and a general ideal of self-reliance, and that concentrated attention for a short time makes for rapid progress. Certain specific helps are provided in teaching children how to study,

[3] Adler, Martha. Mental tests used as a basis for the classification of school children. *Jour. of Educ. Psych.*, 5: January, 1914, 22–28.

for example, study periods in school, even when not assigned by the schedule, that teachers may see which children lack power of concentration and give helpful suggestions to them. The pupils are encouraged to ask questions about their individual difficulties only after they have made a real effort to solve them, and spontaneous effort at accomplishment and comprehension is looked upon as much more valuable than what is done at the teacher's detailed direction.[4]

With this reference to the opinions expressed in educational literature as an introduction, we may undertake a more detailed consideration of the adaptation of method to the distinctive needs of supernormal children. So closely, however, is the question of method connected with that of the characteristics of the teacher that we are perhaps justified in delaying the main issue for a moment in order to make way for some consideration of the qualities which should be sought for in choosing a teacher for a special room of gifted children.

The Teacher

It is but expressing a truism to say that the most retarded pupils are those who are naturally brightest. Almost any teacher who is possessed of the requisite amount of patience can develop a dull pupil to a level relatively near the limit of his ability, but teachers who do not at times retard the brightest members of their classes are rare. Efficient teaching is absolutely necessary if the ablest pupils are to make full use of their powers. Again, any marked departure from the usual program is likely to fail unless the teacher or other authority who has it in charge is forceful and intelligent, and able to command the respect, not only of the pupils but also of the patronizing community in general; and under present conditions a special room for gifted children represents such a departure.

Efficiency in teaching depends upon broad scholarship, adequate preparation, and strong personality, all of which are of prime importance for the kind of work which we are considering. The teacher, in order to be successful in instructing very bright children, must be well-grounded in educational theory and professional knowledge. She must know how to adapt her instruction to the varying needs of

[4] Patterson, M. Rose. A preparatory center in Baltimore; William Rhinehart School No. 52. *Atlantic Educ. Jour.*, 12: January, 1917, 234–238.

her pupils. She must be able to work out a definite lesson plan, in order that both she and the pupils may have an exact understanding of just what is to be done, and waste no time in aimless floundering. She must have the ability to discern relative values and to lift important topics into prominence from the mass of details. No matter how much experience she may have had, she must still preserve the experimental attitude and be capable of noticing wherein her methods must differ from those which she would use under ordinary circumstances; and must remember that many of the conventional ideas of method and technique that obtain in ordinary teaching do not apply to gifted children in a special room, especially since their initiative is so marked. In a word, she must have so profited by professional training as to make it possible for her to recognize the special pedagogical and psychological problems connected with her work.

The wealth of associations which bright children possess, and their quickness in forming others, are features which often make them a source of real difficulty in ordinary schoolrooms and for ordinary teachers. The teacher in the special room for such children, if she is to command the respect of her pupils or cause them to work up to the limit of their powers, must have had a broad general training and a wide range of information. So far as the children in our experimental room were concerned, they did a great deal of outside reading, much of which was more mature in character than the reading of ordinary children of the same age. This resulted in the asking of a great many questions, which covered a broad field. Of course, it is hardly possible that even the best-informed teacher would be able to dispose of all the questions brought to her by a score of very bright children, but she should be able to answer a reasonable number of them and should know where to look for information to answer most of the remainder.

No less important is the matter of personality. To choose a teacher for capable children on the basis of scholarship alone, placing them in charge of a normal-school or college graduate of weak personality and slender teaching resources is to invite disaster. In order to develop the powers of gifted children to their fullest capacity, the teacher of those children must possess an individuality strong enough to challenge those powers. Energy and enthusiasm on the part of the teacher are needed in any schoolroom, but nowhere are they so much needed as in the education of bright children. A lack of them makes the development of self-reliance, industry, and initiative among the pupils almost an impossibility.

The qualities which have been discussed above are, it must be admitted, precisely those qualities which make for good teaching in any room, special or regular. So far as these factors go, none of them is the exclusive property of the teacher of capable pupils. The point that is made here, however, is that gifted children require an especially strong teacher—one who ranks high in scholarship, preparation, and personality—and that, whereas a teacher of lower rank in any of these particulars might do very well in an ordinary room, she would not be capable of securing adequate results in a room such as that upon which this study is based.

Method—

What is true of the teacher is also true of method of the special room. None of the methods which are to be described could be said at all times to be out of place in an ordinary schoolroom; but it is true that some methods, more than others, must characterize the instruction of supernormal children, while other methods must receive more emphasis than would be placed upon them in teaching ordinary children in regular rooms.

The most common modification of method which was reported in my correspondence with supervising officers and teachers of special rooms for gifted children, is *a reduction in the amount of drill*. To the question on this point answers were secured from 20 persons actually engaged in supervising, or giving instruction to, such rooms or classes. In all but four instances there was reported a marked decrease in the amount and relative importance of drill-work, as compared with ordinary schoolroom procedure. Two of these four exceptions came from special teachers of arithmetic, one from a teacher of grammar, and one from a room-teacher giving instruction in all the common branches. Eleven teachers reported a lessening of drill in all subjects; history received specific mention three times in this connection; geography, spelling, and arithmetic were each mentioned twice; bookkeeping once, and "memory-work" once. The most common estimate of the amount of this decrease was 50 per cent. A few put it at one third or one fourth, but the typical answer was "50 per cent in all subjects." One departmental teacher of arithmetic, who teaches both a bright group and an average group, reported that for some time she had been making a careful study of this particular question, and had been keeping a record of the drill-time in each of the two groups. As a result, she found that the time spent in drill with the bright class was just 48 per cent of that in the ordinary class.

A priori, since gifted children grasp principles and concepts more quickly than ordinary children do, not so much drill is necessary in their education as in that of children of ordinary ability. While gifted children must have a certain amount of drill in the skill subjects, care must be taken that they are not required to drudge through long lists of grammatical or arithmetical exercises in order to 'fasten' principles which are already well understood and known by them. The very fact that the bright child is quicker to see things than other children are, goes to indicate that he needs less drill than they do. Experimental evidence is at hand to show that practice increases differences in performance (see Chapter V), and it is a corollary to this that practice is more efficient in the case of able children, and hence less of it is needed to attain any set standard.

One of the teachers who had charge of a 5th-grade class from which a number of the brightest pupils had been selected for the experimental room, and who kept the same class as a 6th grade the next year, remarked to the author that the removal of these pupils had made much more drill necessary in her room. Similar opinions were expressed by the other 5th-grade and 6th-grade teachers whose best pupils had been transferred to the special room. Obviously this indicates that under ordinary circumstances teachers are misled by the performance of bright pupils and give less drill than ordinary children need; or, if they spend time for the drill which is needed by average and dull children they waste the bright pupils' time. All in all, the evidence goes to show that the practice of greatly reducing the amount of drill, which is shown above to obtain quite generally in the instruction of gifted children, is readily justified.

Formal review is only another form of drill, and what has been said in the discussion of drill will apply to review also. In the ordinary schoolroom it quite often happens that the teacher will resort to a period of drill, or to a formal review, simply for the purpose of filling up time which otherwise she would not know what to do with. The author's experience in observing, and teaching in, the special room convinced him that for such children the most efficient kind of drill is a short and very intensive one, and that there should be rather frequent reviews of that character, instead of less frequent, more formal, and longer ones. In such a room neither drill nor review should be given unless at a suitable time, for a clearly understood reason, and after careful planning, and never for the purpose of simply using up time; and as less drill is necessary for gifted children, so also is less review needful.

Aside from decreasing the amount of review and drill, the most frequently reported change in method is a *lessened amount of explanation*, including lessened attention to detail in the development of a new topic. This was mentioned as a leading feature in the adaptation of method by 12 out of 21 persons from whom information was obtained. The following is a typical statement: "Explanation doesn't have to be entered into so minutely, or have to be repeated as with ordinary pupils. They grasped so much more quickly that time was saved thereby." Said another: "They get it at one 'exposure.'" One teacher estimated that bright pupils require from a third to a half the amount of explanation necessary in teaching ordinary ones, and another expressed the figure as 55 per cent.

Since one of the chief purposes in the establishment of special rooms for gifted children is that they be given the opportunity to work as diligently as ordinary children have to work to get their tasks accomplished, it will be readily seen that too much explanation on the part of the teacher would defeat one of the chief aims of such a room. Again, if the program of the special room involves a saving in time, economy in teaching must be featured, as well as economy in learning. Any time, then, which is spent by the teacher in explaining what is already perfectly known by the pupils or in considering details which are of no importance or which could easily be worked out by the pupils themselves, contributes to the defeat of another important aim.

A common form of over-explanation consists in giving *too much attention to illustration*. The danger of this, even in an ordinary room, has been so well pointed out by Professor Adams that I cannot forbear quoting the following paragraph from one of his works,[5] especially since it so well applies to the teaching of bright children:

[5] Adams, J. *Exposition and Illustration in Teaching*, p. 395.

> ". . . There is the danger of over-illustration. Some teachers seem to regard it as an established principle that every point that arises must be illustrated, whether it offers any difficulty or not. What is perfectly clear already needs no illustration as a matter of exposition. A straightforward statement of fact dealing with elements that come well within the pupil's range should not be illustrated, so long as the teacher's purpose at the time is only to get the pupil to understand. Indeed, it is possible that by illustrating what requires no illustration the teacher may cause needless difficulties to arise, especially in the minds of the more eager and attentive pupils. Accustomed to attach a meaning to all that the teacher says, such pupils are apt to think that since he makes so much of the point he is laboring, there must be something in it which they do not yet perceive, and they may grope about for a meaning that is not there."

A mistake which is very likely to be made by the teacher who is placed in charge of a room of gifted pupils for the first time, is to forget *the relative importance of details.* This often occurs because the teacher, finding her pupils able to assimilate a great variety of facts in a comparatively short space of time and seeing great possibilities in the direction of thoroughness, is carried away by that as an ideal, and in her enthusiasm expects her pupils to master every detail which she places before them or which is found in their textbooks, without regard to the relative value of those details. This results in a waste of time and a dissipation of energy. Successful teaching in a special room for bright children must take into account the relative importance of the different topics and make a proportionate division of time. Instead of an encyclopedic treatment of the content subjects, there should be an intensive study of the main topics, supported by many of the details as secondary. In mastering the main topics, bright students will acquire most of the important details spontaneously, but the teacher must be able to distinguish between first-rate and tenth-rate facts in making her assignments and drawing up her lesson-plans.

Another prominent feature of method as adapted to gifted children, is provision for the *development of initiative, self-reliance, and free expression.* These characteristics, of course, have their place in the ordinary schoolroom, but it is in a room of the type which we are describing that they are capable of their fullest development and must receive the greatest emphasis. Many of the teachers with whom I have corresponded have mentioned the use of these traits, and some have furnished me with concrete examples of how they have been enabled to develop a spirit of self-reliance in their pupils and to make it contribute to the work of the school. Thus one says: "The children are required to get information for themselves through silent reading more than ordinary children of this grade (4b), and emphasis is placed upon their ability to discuss what they have read." Another says: "The children take more initiative. They use the material we have at hand more freely." Another: "Far less explaining is necessary, for these children are able to help themselves and they often work out new subjects in grammar and arithmetic. This is the most successful side of my work."

The following paragraph is quoted from the letter of a teacher of a special room for bright children in the Bigelow School, of Boston.

> "In presenting a subject I have been able to dispense with detailed explanations which I have found necessary in regular grade work. The children are quick to grasp a new idea, and to apply previously taught principles. Also the children do more, and I less, of the work than is possible in a regular grade. For instance, in the matter of history—after the children have been trained how to study, I assign a subject. The child studies the subject as a whole, selects what to him are the essentials, and presents them to the class. He must have reasons for his selection, and knowledge enough to answer any question. Dependence on self is the thing we strive to cultivate."[6]

One of the best examples of the development of initiative on the part of school children that has come under the author's immediate observation was in the "opportunity class" under the care of Miss Jessie B. Marshall, of the Louisville, Kentucky, Normal School. This class, which has been described in an earlier part of this study,[7] was composed of very bright children from the fourth grade. In a geography lesson upon the hard-wood lumber industry of Kentucky, one of the boys took a pointer, went to the map, and gave a very well-planned and coherent discussion of the hard-wood timber region of Kentucky, the different varieties of trees found there, and the

[6] Letter from Miss S. H. Lynch, Bigelow School, Boston.

[7] See Chapter II.

methods of putting the lumber upon the market. Opportunity was given to the class to ask him questions, most of which were promptly answered. At the conclusion of his discussion, he took charge of the class, asking them questions connected with the day's lesson, so that to all intents and purposes he taught that lesson to his fellow-pupils. The same method was used in an arithmetic class, where another boy, who had been previously appointed for that purpose, dictated original problems to the class, oversaw their solution, corrected the mistakes, and gave help to such members of the class as seemed to be in need of it.

These three things—lessened drill, lessened explanation, and augmented initiative—according to the reports which I have received, are the most prominent features of method as adapted to the peculiar situation of a special room for gifted children. In addition to these there are at least two other important principles which have been mentioned by a few teachers, and which have been made use of in our own experimental room.

The first of these, for lack of a better name, I shall call the "*principle of application*," meaning by that the endeavor to encourage the pupils in all possible ways to make use of the knowledge already acquired by them, in the acquisition of more knowledge. In my experience in teaching these children, I found the step of 'application' following the development of a principle, a very easy one for them to make, and they were encouraged to apply each principle to as wide a field as possible. When it could be done, arithmetical principles were taught as closely as possible in connection with their applications. To illustrate, in the textbook which was used in arithmetic in the 5th grade, cancellation was treated as a separate topic, having a section devoted to an explanation of the principle involved and a list of problems for drill. But before this section of the textbook had been reached, opportunity was seen for the introduction of cancellation, and it was explained to the class, somewhat casually at first, as a method of saving time in connection with a certain problem. This process was repeated, until after the class had seen the method used a few times they were perfectly able to use it for themselves, and consequently it was possible to omit almost all of the section of the textbook which was devoted to that subject. To make sure that the children are making use of the knowledge which they have, the teacher should allow the pupils to tell what they know about the subject under discussion, even if they go into details which are in advance of the lesson for the day. The conventional treatment of the child who "goes ahead of the lesson" in his recitation is to restrain him. It has been our experience, however, that much advantage is secured by allowing children to anticipate advance matter in this way. It prevents waste of time later in teaching the children what they already know, and it gives the teacher opportunity to discover what connections already formed in the child's mind are available as means of approach to new material.

Another feature of the instruction in the experimental room has been the conscious effort to *teach as much as possible by principles* instead of by more or less detached facts. For instance, the 5th-grade textbook in geography treated the difference in rainfall on the sides of the Coast Ranges of the western United States by simply mentioning the fact, without explaining the principle of the loss of moisture during the passage of clouds from the sea over a mountain range. This principle was, however, developed by the class, so that a few weeks later, when the geography of the Amazon valley was being studied, the class was able to deduce the direction of the prevailing winds from the text's simple statement of the difference in rainfall on the sides of the Andes. Similar methods were used in physiology, and, indeed, wherever possible.

In addition to what has already been said concerning special adaptations of method in the experimental room, a few other features may be mentioned. There was a persistent attempt to take into account the relative importance of the different topics and portions of subject matter and to make a corresponding distribution of time and emphasis among them. Perhaps the greatest saving of time has been effected by the quickness with which the children learn, which has made it possible to dispense with the long explanations that would otherwise be necessary. There was a persistent attempt, therefore, to get at the root of the matter as quickly as possible, without wasting any time in needless explanation. When it was found, as it often was, that the pupils were already perfectly familiar with a principle for whose development the course of study or the textbook provided an extended amount of formal drill, the drill was correspondingly shortened. Again, it was often discovered that the children already knew enough about an advance topic to render unnecessary any detailed development of it.

As nearly as we could estimate, the amount of drill was by these methods lessened about 50 per cent in all subjects except formal grammar, where the reduction was about 30 per cent. In place of having all the pupils solve all the problems given to illustrate each topic in arithmetic, approximately a third of them were omitted. Much use was made of the practice of having one pupil work an example at the board where it would command the concentrated attention of the class. Many original problems were set and solved by the pupils; and very often, in order to provide problems difficult enough to call forth real effort, they were assigned from textbooks of a grade higher than the one in use. In particular more "thought problems" were given.

In geography and history, the reviews by questions furnished in the book were frequently replaced by reports given by members of the class upon supplementary readings covering the same ground. The principle of application was also often made use of in review in different subjects, and was so used whenever it seemed advisable, whether at the beginning or at the close of a lesson or during its development. In reviewing history in the 6th grade, each child gave a report worked out by himself, on two separate periods. These reports were well-developed; the manner of presenting the facts were in most cases very good, and original comments and comparisons were made.

The teacher found it possible to correlate lessons to a much greater degree than in an ordinary room, and it was also possible to do more supplementary work. Outlines of lessons were frequently worked out by the pupils. Sometimes this was done in advance by pupils appointed for the purpose, and their outlines then used before the class as the basis of the assignment. Much less testing was necessary in developing a lesson with these children than would have been required with ordinary ones, and our selected pupils were easily led to develop topics by wholes. Since it was possible for the teacher to find many more points of contact with the interests of these children, it was much easier for her to make the work concrete and real. She did not find it nearly so difficult to stimulate their interest as to keep it within due bounds.

Discipline

Closely connected with methods of teaching is *the question of discipline.* I have answers from twelve teachers of bright children to the question: "Does the instruction of bright children present any peculiar problems of discipline?" The practically unanimous testimony of these teachers is to the effect that, far from presenting any problem, discipline in the gifted room need hardly be considered. One teacher says that bright children must be kept very busy, and are frequently inattentive because they already know what is being explained. Another says that the only difficulty in this respect is a tendency to interrupt one another in discussion, and that this is probably due to their interest in the subject. Some typical answers are quoted: "It is the most orderly school I have ever taught." "We have no trouble with regularity of attendance, punctuality, or discipline. We try very hard to make our class an inspiration to the school." "I never had better order and it is the same whether I am in or out of the room. I feel sure better discipline in all schools could be secured if pupils were divided according to their ability." Our experience with our own group of bright children was quite in line with this testimony, for at no time did the question of discipline need any consideration. Although one of the 6th-grade boys had been a source of trouble during the previous year, after he was transferred to the special room his conduct was uniformly good. While this change may have been due to other causes, rather than to his being placed in the special room, the fact is not without significance. An exactly similar case was reported to me from the class in the Louisville Normal School, and I am very strongly led to believe that the conduct in school of a boy who is both bright and mischievous would be greatly improved by putting him into a special room where he might have opportunity to exercise his powers and to form habits of industry and attention.

Because it is argued by some that the segregation of bright children in special rooms tends to develop priggishness, clannishness, egotism, and vanity, and because the possession of such undesirable characteristics by bright children would greatly modify the teacher's method of dealing with them, information was sought as to whether bright children possess these traits in any inordinate degree, and whether there is any noticeable tendency toward their development among those who have been placed in special rooms. Opinions upon these points were secured from ten teachers of these rooms. Eight of them report that their pupils are not snobbish and priggish, and that segregation has not developed undemocratic attitudes or sentiments. Two say that in their classes the children do exhibit these egotistic traits; one that she notices them "in a marked degree." Both these teachers taught the same group of children, however, one as a special teacher of history, the other of geography, in a school under departmental organization. An interesting paragraph from one of the letters in answer to this question is quoted:

> "I feel sure that egotism and priggishness are not developed, but only a proper amount of personal pride to do well. They are just ordinary, healthy children, and are just like normal children, with perhaps the exception of their fondness for reading. I notice in the playground they enjoy each other's company, but they are not clannish about it."[8]

Terman secured extensive information concerning 31 very bright children from their teachers. Twenty-two of these children were reported as not spoiled or vain, five as spoiled, and two as somewhat spoiled. No statement was made about the remaining two. As a result of his inquiry, Terman says:

> "According to testimony of their teachers; such children are fully as likely to be healthy as average children; their ability is far more often general than special; they are studious above the average; really serious moral faults are not common among them; they are nearly always socially adaptable; are sought often as playmates and companions; they are leaders far oftener than other children; and notwithstanding their many really superior qualities, they are seldom vain or spoiled."[9]

So far as the pupils in our room at Urbana were concerned, in general they presented the appearance of ordinary children and had the same social characteristics, so that the atmosphere of the room was entirely normal. One or two mild cases of egotism were noted, but these could be explained by conditions at home and had been developed before the children entered the experimental room. So far as our

[8] Letter from Miss Helen M. Richardson, George Putnam School, Boston.

[9] Terman, L. M. Mental hygiene of exceptional children, *Pedagogical Seminary*, 22:529–537.

experience goes, it agrees with the burden of evidence that bright children are not made vain or conceited by placing them in a room organized especially to meet their peculiar needs. It is perfectly legitimate for able children to feel an honest pride in their achievements, and there is actually *less* chance for them to acquire a feeling of superiority in a room in which they are thrown into competition with their equals, than in an ordinary room where they stand out as clearly superior to their schoolmates.

Summary

In this chapter we have examined the distinctive features of that special method of instruction to which gifted pupils are entitled, on the basis of the results of the mental and educational tests which have previously been described.

It has been shown that for a special room for bright children is demanded an exceptionally able teacher—one who possesses broad scholarship, adequate professional preparation, and a strong and commanding personality.

According to the testimony of those who are engaged in the actual work of instruction in such rooms, the chief modifications of method which are being made use of in practice are the lessening of drill, the lessening in amount and detail of explanation, and greater provision for initiative on the part of the pupils. Other important features are the provision of opportunities for the pupils to make use of the knowledge which they have already gained, and the emphasizing of broad, underlying principles rather than more or less unrelated facts. The difference in importance of the various topics and portions of subject matter demands a corresponding difference in amount of time devoted to them and in emphasis placed upon them.

There are no peculiar problems of discipline connected with the administration of a special room for gifted children, nor do the pupils of such rooms exhibit any inordinate amount of clannishness, priggishness, vanity, or egotism.

CHAPTER VIII

GENERAL SUMMARY AND RECOMMENDATIONS

The experimental part of this study has demonstrated that children representing the top tenth of the school population of the middle grades, on a proper basis of selection, are able to accomplish two years of the ordinary school work of those grades in one year, under a mediocre teacher and with average conditions of supervision and equipment, without any undue strain or any depreciation in the quality of their work when measured by the standard educational scales and tests as well as by the methods ordinarily used in the school. It has also been shown that gifted children excel in regularity of attendance, and that their segregation in a special room practically eliminates the problem of discipline and does not tend to develop in them egotism, vanity, clannishness, or priggishness. The results of the practice test described in the text confirm the opinion of previous investigators that practice, so far from decreasing individual differences, tends, on the contrary, to increase them. Tests in the fundamental subjects of the school course have quite uniformly shown that the children in the experimental room in the Leal School, taken as a group, have an ability equal to that of ordinary children a year older than they, and the same advancement was shown in the results of the mental tests. All the evidence at hand points to the fact that the mental differences between superior and average children are of such a nature that in their instruction a special adaptation of method is necessary, the leading features of which have just been indicated.

In summarizing the more specific details of our study, it is desirable to offer certain definite suggestions concerning the organization and conduct of special rooms for gifted children. These recommendations are offered upon the basis of the author's observation of the work of the experimental room throughout the year, upon the results of the educational and psychological tests which were applied by the other investigators, and upon present practice in rooms of the same kind as ascertained by correspondence with teachers and school officials in charge of them.

Recommendations

1. *The enrollment of a special room for gifted pupils should represent a selection of approximately the top ten per cent of the ordinary school population in the grades which are to be represented.*

To put this statement into terms of the intelligence quotient; enrollment in the special room should be limited to children who possess an intelligence quotient of at least 115. In practice this would mean the segregation of approximately the top tenth.

2. *Health should be an important factor in the selection of the pupils.*

While, as has been shown, the pupils of our own room were under no undue strain and suffered no impairment of health, it may readily be seen that the purposes for which a special room is organized, and the methods by which those purposes are attained, are such as to render it inadvisable for highly nervous or sickly children to be included in its membership. This consideration was, of course, taken into account by those who selected our pupils, so that the children in the experimental room represented at least average conditions of health and physique.

3. *The method of selecting gifted pupils should be by mental tests, not by teachers' estimates of the pupils' ability or estimates by school administrators from school marks.*

An examination of the tables of results of the mental tests which have been described in Chapter VI will show that a few individuals consistently made low scores. These same individuals made low scores in the educational tests, and, likewise, if the selection had been made on the basis of the possession of an intelligence quotient of at least 115, instead of on the opinion of the school authorities, they are just the ones that would have not been admitted to the special class. It is the presence of these pupils that in large part accounts for the wide range of scores that our selected group shows in the various tables. It often happens that a certain superficial glibness passes for intelligence to such an extent that a teacher is readily deceived, or that a good memory conceals the lack of ability to reason. These, or other, factors may creep in to warp a teacher's judgment of the abilities of any particular pupil, with the result that when the selection is made for a special class on the basis of a teacher's opinion, whether expressed in class marks or otherwise, it may readily happen, as it did in this instance, that some pupils are selected who, although they have succeeded in obtaining high marks in their school work when proceeding at the usual rate, are able only with difficulty to keep up with the natural pace of those who are really mentally fit for segregation as superior pupils. Mental tests, on the other hand, do furnish an impersonal and scientific method of selection, which takes into account only intellectual ability.[1]

4. *The teacher of a special room for gifted children must possess a large fund of general information.*

Broad general information is necessary in order to meet with the wide range of questions which are the result of the wealth of associations which bright children possess and the extended field of their interests, as well as to make use of points of contact which would not be available in the instruction of ordinary children and which obviously ought to be capitalized.

5. *The teacher must have had adequate foundation in the theory and practice of education.*

This is essential in order that economy in teaching and in learning be brought about through definite plans of work, and through the ability on the part of the teacher to understand and carry out those special adaptations of method which are suited to the education of gifted children.

6. *The teacher must be characterized by energy, enthusiasm, and an inspiring personality.*

In order to develop in these children the necessary habits of self-reliance, industry, and initiative, the teacher, on her part, must exhibit energy and enthusiasm, and must have a personality such as to inspire her pupils to put forth their best efforts and to challenge them to summon all their powers.

7. *The teacher in charge of a special room should be carried along with it in its advancement, and should remain with it as long as it retains its organization.*

[1] Professor Whipple has recently placed on the market a special pamphlet of group tests for the selection of gifted children, particularly in the 4th, 5th and 6th grades.

This arrangement makes for economy of time, in that it becomes unnecessary for the pupils, at the beginning of each year, to adjust themselves to the characteristics, methods, and requirements of a new teacher; nor is any time lost by the teacher in making the acquaintance of a new set of pupils. It also permits greater freedom in the organization of subject matter from year to year in the course.

8. *The special room should be equipped with movable desks, and should be well supplied with maps, charts, globes, pictures, and other aids to study.*

The use of movable desks gives much more freedom of movement to the pupils, and makes possible much greater variety in conducting the exercises of the school. If the pupils have access to books for supplementary reading, maps, globes, and other illustrative material, their study will be more independent, and they will have opportunity to learn how to work for themselves.

9. *In the special room for gifted children, drill should be decreased by about 50 per cent.*

Correspondence with teachers shows this to be a prevalent practice in rooms of this kind, and corroborative evidence has been furnished by the work of the experimental room. Results of learning tests indicate that practice is more efficient in the case of those who already possess high initial ability.

10. *Likewise, explanation should be reduced about 50 per cent in amount, and needs to be given in much less detail than to ordinary pupils.*

This is also the common practice in special rooms for gifted pupils. It is justified by the quickness with which the children learn and by their greater ability in perceiving relationships.

11. *Emphasis should be placed upon the development of the pupils' initiative.*

A prominent feature in the education of bright children is the increase of opportunity for the exercise of initiative on their part, with a consequent insistence upon self-reliance and free expression.

12. *Much use should be made of the 'principle of application.'*

In carrying out this principle, pupils must be encouraged in all possible ways to make immediate and practical application of what they have learned, in the acquisition of new knowledge and in the other activities of the schoolroom. In particular, the teacher may often very advantageously make use of this principle in provision for review.

13. *Instruction should be as much as possible by broad, underlying principles, rather than by detached facts.*

This is an important principle in all teaching, but it can be realized to a much greater extent with bright children than with ordinary ones, and consequently needs to receive greater emphasis in their instruction.

14. *An important feature of the teacher's method is the development of a proper perspective of the material of instruction.*

This implies the ability to estimate the relative importance of the different topics and pieces of subject matter in order to make a proper distribution of time and energy among them and to insure that the more important topics receive the greater attention.

15. *The teacher of the special room for bright children need pay but little attention to discipline, beyond seeing to it that the pupils have work enough to keep them busy.*

The testimony of those who are engaged in giving instruction to special groups of bright children is practically unanimous to the effect that no disciplinary troubles are encountered. While bright children sometimes cause trouble in ordinary rooms, because of the lack of employment, when they are placed in a room where they have plenty of work to occupy their attention, and where they must exert themselves to keep up with their fellows, their idleness gives place to industry, and they cease to give any trouble on the score of conduct. The only recommendation that needs to be made upon this point, then, is that the teacher see to it that the pupils have work enough to occupy their time.

16. *If any of the pupils in the special room seem to be developing egotistic tendencies, the teacher should apply the 'social check.'*

Contrary to the impression entertained by some, segregation of superior children does not inevitably develop in them undemocratic ideas and attitudes. Quite the opposite, for in fact there is *more* opportunity for the development of the feeling of superiority on the part of the bright child in the regular room than in the special room. Under ordinary conditions, the bright child stands out conspicuously above his fellows, his superiority is acknowledged by them, often to the point of resentment, and he is keenly aware of it. When a question has gone round the rest of the class without receiving an answer, the teacher turns to him with an air of finality and relief. Such opportunity for display does not come to the child in the special room, for here he is among real competitors, and in place of being always in the lead he must often exert himself to keep up with the rest. Of course, it would not be out of place for a teacher of a special room, as well as any other teacher, to keep close watch for the beginnings of vanity and egotism in order that she may promptly check them. This can often be done by comparing the work of the child who needs to be thus corrected with that of some other pupil of superior, or at least equal, ability in that particular line. It is actually easier for a teacher to hold such tendencies in check in a room where the pupils are of about equal ability than in a room where the bright children are conspicuous by their superiority over their classmates.

17. *Corresponding to the special adaptations of method, there should be a readjustment of emphasis in subject matter.*

Modification of methods of instruction must perforce bring about modification in subject matter. Corresponding to the lessened amount of drill, there will be a lessening in the number of problems and exercises in the formal subjects. Less attention should be given to details of secondary importance, and more attention to necessary principles. Much of the purely explanatory matter in the textbooks may be passed over lightly or even omitted. It was found, in our experimental room, that the children often knew much of the matter ahead of them in the course of study, and this made it possible for that material to be passed over rapidly. Especially did this happen when a new volume in a series of textbooks in the same subject was taken up. For instance, the advanced textbook in geography, which the special 6th grade began to study at about the middle of the year, began with a review of the definitions and principles which the pupils had learned in their study of the intermediate book. Since it was found that the children were already perfectly familiar with practically all this material, this portion of the book was used only for a rapid review, instead of being made the subject of definite and extended assignments, as would have been the case if the matter had been entirely new. Exactly the same thing took place in 5th-grade arithmetic and 6th-grade language.

18. *The teacher of a special room for gifted children should be allowed wide latitude in modifying the course of study to fit the purpose of the room and the needs of the pupils.*

The author's work with the experimental room during the year thoroughly convinced him that a great deal of freedom should be allowed the teacher of a gifted room in following the conventional course of study. The investigators all felt that from the standpoint of the experiment, a considerable amount of time was lost in doing work which could be justified only on the ground of preparation for the somewhat rigid requirements of a conservative school system. The fact that we were not allowed to alter the sequence of any of the branches of subject matter seriously interfered with our efforts to condense the regular course of study for the two years into an economical and efficient one-year course. If a teacher of the type which has been recommended is once secured, she should be left in comparative freedom to select what she considers the essential parts of the course of study, and to present them in the order which is best adapted to the needs of her class. The time saved by these methods would afford opportunity to add a considerable quantity of outside material of a cultural nature, much of which might well be supplied by the pupils themselves. This added material might include, among many others, such things as extended supplementary reading of standard literature mainly for appreciation, dramatization, pageantry free discussion of the important topics in the news of the day, the collection of newspaper clippings correlating with the work in civics and hygiene, the illustration of history and geography with such relics, costumes, utensils, etc., as are available or can be procured, especially those which the pupils are able to bring, enrichment of the work in history by some consideration of industrial history, study of local city and state industries in connection with the work in geography, and so on through a long list. In some cases it might be possible to take up the study of a foreign language, as was done in the "opportunity class" in the Louisville Normal School, where 4th-grade children were given daily lessons in German, wholly by the conversational method.

Special rooms for gifted children are of two general types. One type, which is the more common, contemplates a saving of time by providing for the more rapid progress of the pupils. The other makes no provision for the saving of time, but makes use of a course of study different from the ordinary one in that it either (*a*) contains more of the same kind of material, or (*b*) includes different material, which is usually of a more cultural nature. Of the second type, the latter arrangement is by far the better. It is subject to one danger, however, in that in the attempt to add cultural material, the course may be so diluted as to defeat one of the most important purposes of such rooms, namely, the provision of opportunity for gifted children to learn what hard mental work is. This danger, however, is not inherent in the scheme and may very easily be avoided.

Although most of the special rooms for gifted children now in operation have a course of study so arranged as to make it possible for the pupils to do three years' work in two, this study has shown that bright children of the 5th and 6th grades can do two years' work in one, and the same gain in time has been accomplished in one or two other rooms of the kind. By lessening the amount of drill, decreasing the amount of explanation, and, on the side of subject matter, omitting or passing rapidly over what is already known or of relative unimportance, enough time can be saved so that all of the essential topics of the two years' work can be mastered in one. There will be time enough left, in addition, to make possible the introduction of a considerable amount of cultural material of the kind mentioned above, by which the course will be enriched and made to connect more completely with the lives of the individual pupils.

CHAPTER IX

BIBLIOGRAPHY ON THE PSYCHOLOGY AND PEDAGOGY OF GIFTED CHILDREN

This bibliography, which is not to be regarded as complete, attempts to give a fairly comprehensive list of references dealing, in various ways, with questions concerning the mentality of gifted children, as well as their training.

Adler, Martha. Mental tests used as a basis for the classification of school children. *J. Educ. Psych.*, 5:1914, 22–28.

Alderman, L. R. Effort to make the school fit the needs of the exceptional child. *Proc. N. E. A.*, 1914, 830–835.

Aley, J. A. Care of exceptional children in the grades. *Proc. N. E. A.*, 1910, 881–886.

Anon. A class of exceptional children. *School*, 28: June 7, 1917, 409.

Answer to Correspondent. How can we give to the brighter child the benefit of his better endowment. *American School*, 2: May, 1916, 156.

Becht, A. A. Bright pupils and dull pupils. *J. Educ.*, 79: 1914, 395–6.

Berkhan, O. Otto Pöhler, das frühlesende Braunschweiger Kind. *Zeits. f. Kinderforschung*, 15:1910, 166–171.

Berkhan, O. Das Wunderkind, Christian H. Heineken. *Zeits. f. Kinderforschung*, 15:1910, 225–229.

Berle, A. A. *Teaching in the Home*. New York, 1915.

Berry C. S. Special classes in Michigan for mentally exceptional children, in *Rept. Supt. Public Instruction*, Michigan, 1914–15, especially 57–75.

Bliss, D. C. The application of standard measurements to school administration. *Fifteenth Yearbook of the National Society for the Study of Education, Part I*, 1916, 69–78.

Boggs, Anita U. A plea for the forward child. *The Child*, 2: Oct. 1911, 45–47.

Boston, Mass., School Committee, Annual Reports, 1913, 1914.

Breitweiser, J. V. The case for the gifted child. *Colorado School Journal,* 28: April, 1913, 20–22.

Bruce, H. A. Lightning calculators. *McClure's Mag.*, 39: 1912, 586–596.

Bruce, H. A. New ideas in child training. *Amer. Mag.*, 72: July, 1911, 286–294.

Bruce, H. A. Story of Karl Witte. *Outlook*, 100: 1912, 211–218.

Burk, Caroline F. Promotion of bright and slow children. *Educ. Rev.*, 19: 1900, 296–302.

Burnell, Elizabeth F. Instruction in mathematics for gifted pupils. *Ped. Sem.*, 24: 1917, 569–583.

Cambridge, Mass., School Committee, Annual Reports, 1908, 1910.

-Cautley, E. The precocious child. *The Child*, 9: Aug , 1919, 481–486.

-Christenson, D. H. Changes in the course of study and school organization to meet the varying capacities of children. *Proc. N. E. A.*, 1912, 355–368.

Clerk F. E. The Arlington plan of grouping pupils according to ability in the Arlington High School. *Sch. Rev.*, 25: 1917, 26–47.

Cleveland, Elizabeth. Report of Director of the Special Advanced Class, in Annual Report, Board of Education, Detroit, Mich., 1916, p. 94.

- Collicott, J. G. The bright pupil. *Proc. N. E. A.* 1915, 457–462. (Discussion, 462–466.)

Cooper, H. E. Another study of retardation. *Educ. Admin. and Superv.*, 5: April, 1919, 177–183.

Coy, Genevieve. The mentality of a gifted child. *J. Applied Psych.*, 2: 1918, 299–307.

Davidson, H. A. The gift of genius. *J. of Ped.*, 16:1904, 281–297.

Deffenbaugh, W. S. Current progress in schools of cities of 25,000 population or less. U. S. Com. Ed., Report, 1914, Vol. I.

- Dolbear, Katherine. Precocious children. *Ped. Sem.*, 19:1912, 461–491.

Donovan M. E., and Thorndike, E. L. Improvement in a practice experiment under school conditions. *Amer. Jour. Psych.*, 24:July, 1913, 426–428.

Dooley, Lucile. Psychoanalytic studies of genius. *Amer. Jour. Psych.*, 27:1916, 363–416.

Dorr, Rheta. The child that is different. *Century*, 83:1912, 924–930.

Downes, F. E. Seven years with unusually gifted pupils. *Psych. Clinic.*, 6:1912, 13–17.

Dutton, C. F. Management of precocious children. *Cleveland Medical Mag.*, 13:1898, 143–151.

Eike, P. V. The most learned boy in the world. *Amer. Mag.*, 81: March, 1916, 52.

Eliot, C. W. Educational changes needed for the war and subsequent peace. *Education*, 38: May, 1918, 655–658.

Ellis, H. A. *A Study of British Genius*. 1904.

Ernst, Lucy H. Das jugendliche Genie. *VIme Congress Intern. de Psychologie*, 1910, 674–684.

Fleischmann, F. A boy prodigy and the fourth dimension. *Harper's Weekly*, 104, Jan. 15, 1910, 9.

-Follett, W. Schooling without the school. *Harper's Mag.*, 139: Oct. 1919, 700-708

Galton, F. *Hereditary Genius*, London, 1914.

Garrison, C. G.; Burke, Agnes; and Hollingworth, Leta S. Psychology of a prodigious child. *J. Applied Psych.*, 1:1917, 101–110.

Gates, A. I. Correlation of immediate and delayed recall. *J. Educ. Psych.*, 9: Nov. 1918, 489–496.

Gillette, J. M. The conservation of talent through utilization. *Scientific Monthly*, 1: 1915, 151–164.

-Gillingham, Anna. The bright child and the school. *Jour. Educ. Psych.*, 10: May-June, 1919, 237–252.

Gist, A. S. The acceleration of pupils. *Sch. and Soc.*, 5: Jan. 27, 1917, 116–118.

Goddard, H. H. *Psychology of the Normal and Subnormal*, New York, 1919, 216–7.

Goddard, H. H. Two thousand normal children measured by the Binet measuring scale of intelligence. *Ped. Sem.*, 18: 1911, 232–259.

Gregory, C. Holding pupils in school. *Atlantic Educ. J.*, 2: April, 1916, also in *New Jersey Educ. Bull.* Dec. 1915, Part II.

- Groszmann, M. P. E. *The Exceptional Child*, New York, 1917, especially Ch. VII.

Groszmann, M. P. E. Care of exceptionally bright children. *Educational Foundations*, 26: June, 1915, 587–592. (Also *Med. Rev. of Reviews*, 21: 1915, 212–214; *Scientific Amer. Sup.*, 80: Sep. 11, 1915, 171; and *Mind and Body*, 2: Feb. 1915, 508 ff.

Groszmann, M. P. E. The exceptionally bright child. *Proc. Nat. Assoc. Study and Educ. Exceptional Children*, April, 1910, 103–133.

Guthrie, L. G. Contributions from history and literature to the study of precocious children. *Lancet*, 173:1907, 1592–6.

Hardesty, Annie H. Teaching my boys at home. *Ladies' World*, Jan. 1916, 12.

Harley, H. L. Physical status of the special class for bright children at the University of Pennsylvania summer session, 1912. *Psych. Clinic*, 7: March, 1913, 20–23.

Harris, W. T. Class intervals in the graded schools. *Proc. N. E. A.*, 1900, 323–340.

Harrisburg, Pa. School Committee, Annual Report, 1912.

Hill, D. S. *Notes on the Problems of Extreme Individual Differences in Children of the Public Schools.* New Orleans, 1913, especially pp. 67–72.

Hirsch, W. *Genius and Degeneration.* New York, 1896.

- Hoke, K. J. The public schools and the abnormal child. *Psych. Clinic*, 9: January, 1916, 238–245.

Holmes, W. H. Plans for classification in the public schools. *Ped. Sem.*, 18:1911, 475–502.

Holmes, W. H. Promotion classes for gifted pupils. *J. of Educ.*, 75:1912, 376–379.

Holmes, W. H. *School Organization and the Individual Child.* Worcester, Mass., 1912.

Jones, C. T. Suggestive plan for the study of very bright children. *J. of Educ.*, 85: March, 1917, 290–292.

Jones, E. E. Suggestions from cases of unusually rapid or irregular progress in public schools. *Proc. N. E. A.*, 1912, 640–645.

Kendall, C. N. Modifications in organization necessary to secure suitable recognition of pupils of varying ability. *Proc. N. E. A.*, 1908, 147–152.

Kiernan, J. J. Is genius a sport, a neurosis, or a child potentially developed? *Alienist and Neurologist*, 36: 1915, 165–236, *et. seq.*

Kolbe, P. R. Problem of the competent. *Sch. and Soc.*, 3: March 11, 1916, 378–380.

Lang, A. Genius in children. *N. Amer. Rev.*, 165:January, 1897.

Lee, J. B. Breaking the lock step in our schools. *Educ. Rev.*, 56: Sept. 1918, 149–157.

Lindley, E. H. and Bryan, W. L. An arithmetical prodigy. *Psych. Rev.*, 7:1900, 135 ff.

Louisville, Ky. Board of Education. Sixth Report, 1917, especially pp. 40–44, 81.

Lynch, Ella J. The bright child. *Psych. Clinic*, 4:1910, 141–144.

Macmillan, D. P. The discovery and training of exceptionally bright children, in *The Child in the City*, 1912, pp. 203–212.

McDonald, R. A. F. *Adjustment of School Organization to Various Population Groups.* (Teachers Coll. Contrib. to Educ. No. 75, 1915) especially Ch. xi.

Maennel, B. *The Auxiliary Schools of Germany.* (Eng. trans. Bull. U. S. Bureau Educ., 1907, No. 3.)

Melcher, G. Studies of the bureau of research and efficiency of Kansas City, Mo., in the *Fifteenth Yearbook Nat. Soc. for the Study of Educ.*, 1916, p. 131 ff.

Millard, B. Precocity and genius. *Bookman*, 42: Nov., 1915, 340–345.

Miller, C. A. The study of exceptional children. *Proc. N. E. A.*, 1908, 957–963, especially 958–9.

Miller, G. A. Mathematical prodigies. *Science*, 26: Nov. 8, 1907, p. 628 ff.

Mitchell, F. D. Mathematical prodigies. *Amer. J. Psych.*, 18:1907, 61–143.

Morrison, J. C. The supervisor's use of standard tests of efficiency. *Elem. Sch. J.*, January, 1917.

Mulford, H. J. The human mind. A suggestion as to the constitution of normal, subnormal, and supernormal mind. *Amer. J. Psych.*, 29: July, 1918, 272–290.

Mulrey, Cora L. The rapid advancement class. *Educ. Adm. and Superv.*, 3:1917, 416–419.

Myers, G. C. Broadening the course of study for the brighter children. *Educ. Adm. and Superv.*, 3: Jan. 1917, 33–37.

Neverman, P. F. New Richmond plan of grade promotion. *Amer. Schl. Bd. J.*, 54: Jan., 1917, 38.

Newton, Mass. School Committee, Annual Report, 1913.

Norsworthy, Naomi. Acquisition as related to retention. *J. Educ. Psych.*, 4:1913, 214–218.

Norsworthy, Naomi, and Whitley, Mary T. *The Psychology of Childhood*, New York, 1918, pp. 328–333.

Olerich, H. The cleverest child in the world. *Strand Mag.*, 20: 1900, 130–136. Review in *Ped. Sem.*, 7:1900, 455.

Olerich, H. Das wunderliche Viola Rosalia Olerich. *Körperliche Erziehung*, 9:1913, 323–329.

O'Shea, M. V. Popular misconceptions concerning precocity in children. *Science*, 34:1911, 666–674.

O'Shea, M. V. What Mrs. Stoner did for her child. *McClure's Mag.*, 45: July, 1915, 38–39; 76–77.

Ostwald, W. Grösse Männer. Leipzig, 1909.

Patterson, M. Rose. A preparatory center in Baltimore, William Rinehart School No. 52. *Atlantic Educ. J.*, 12:1917, 234–238.

Petzoldt, J. Die Einwande gegen Sonderschulen f. hervorragend Befähigte. *Neue Jahrbücher f. Päd.*, 28:1911, 1–24.

Petzoldt, J. Drei Thesen über Sonderschulen f. hevorragend Befähigte. *Arbeiten des Bund f. Schulreform*, Nr. 5, 68–74.

Petzoldt, J. Sonderschulen für hervorragend Befähigte. *Neue Jahrbücher f. Päd.*, 14: 1904, 425–456.

Pressey, S. L. and Pressey, L. W. The practical efficiency of a group scale of intelligence. *J. Applied Psych.*, 3: March, 1919, 68–80.

Pyle, W. H. A psychological study of bright and dull pupils. *J. Educ. Psych.*, 6:1915, 151–156.

Pyle, W. H. Retention as related to repetition. *J. Educ. Psych.*, 2:1911, 311–321.

Race, Henrietta V. A study of a class of children of superior intelligence. *J. Educ. Psych.*, 9: Feb. 1918, 91–98.

Rathmann, C. C. The Mannheim system of school organization. *Educ. Rev.*, 53: 1917, 55–60.

Reed, Ivy K. The three R's at four years old. *Atlantic Monthly*, 123: May, 1919, 664–668.

Roberts, J. E. *A Working Scheme of Promotional Efficiency.* Madison, Wis., 1916.

Sakaki, Y. Some studies of so-called abnormally intelligent pupils. *Psych. Clinic.* 6:1912, 18–25.

Schwarz, O. L. *General Types of Superior Men.* Boston, 1917.

Scripture, E. W. Arithmetical prodigies. *Am. J. Psych.*, 4:1891, 1–59.

Search, P. W. *An Ideal School, or Looking Forward.* New York, 1901.

Seashore, C. E. The talented child. *J. Educ. Psych.*, 7:1916, 241–2.

Shaer, I. Special classes for bright children in an English elementary school. *J. Educ. Psych.*, 4:1913, 209–222.

Shearer, W. J. *The Grading of Schools, including a Full Explanation of a Rational Plan of Grading.* New York, 1899.

Sidis, B. *Philistine and Genius.* New York, 1911.

Specht, Louise F. A Terman class in Public School No. 64, Manhattan. *Schl. and Soc.*, 9: Mar. 29, 1919, 393–398.

Stedman, Lulu. An experiment in educational democracy. *Sierra Educ. News*, 15: Oct. 1919, 515-8.

Stern, W. *Die differentielle Psychologie in ihrem Methodischen Grundlagen.* Leipzig, 1911.

Stern, W. The supernormal child. *J. Educ. Psych.*, 2:1911, 143–148 and 181–190.

Stoner, Mrs. Winifred S. How I trained my daughter. *Ladies' World*, July, 1915. (See also numbers for Aug., Sept., and Oct.)

Stoner, Mrs. Winifred S. *Natural Education.* Indianapolis, 1914.

Taylor, J. F. The classification of pupils in elementary algebra. *J. Educ. Psych.*, 9:1918, 361–380.

Terman, L. M. Genius and stupidity. *Ped. Sem.*, 13: 1906, 307–373.

Terman, L. M. *The Intelligence of School Children.* Boston, 1919, especially Chs. x and xi.

Terman, L. M. *The Measurement of Intelligence.* Boston, 1916, especially pp. 95–104.

Terman, L. M. Mental hygiene of exceptional children. *Ped. Sem.*, 22:1915, 529–537

Terman, L. M. Precocious children. *Forum*, 62: 1914, 893–898.

Terman, L. M. Precocity and prematuration. *Amer. J. Psych.*, 16:1905, 145–183.

Terman, L. M. and Anon. An experiment in infant education. *J. Applied Psych.*, 2:1918, 219–228.

Ullrich, R. Sonderschulen f. hervorragend Befähigte? *Neue Jahrbücher f. Päd.*, 16: 1905, 425–440.

Unrich, Flora. A year's work in a 'superior' class. *Psych. Clinic*, 5:1912, 245–250.

Van Sickle, J. H. Report of commission on provision for exceptional children in the public schools. *Elem. Sch. Teacher*, 10: April, 1910, 357–366; also in *Proc. N. E. A.*, 1910, 321–335.

Van Sickle, J. H. Rept. Com. on Provision for Exceptional Children in the Public Schools. *Proc. N. E. A.*, 1908, pp. 350–1.

Van Sickle, Witmer, and Ayres. Provision for Exceptional Children in Public Schools. *U. S. Bur. Educ. Bull. No. 461* (1911, No. 14).

Wallin, J. E. W. *The Mental Health of the School Child.* New Haven, 1914, especially pp. 104, 128–9, 372–8.

Ward, L. F. *Applied Sociology.* New York, 1906, especially Chs. 8, 9, 10.

Washburn, W. C. Special provision for the bright pupil. *Pop. Educ.*, 30: Sept., 1912, 5–6.

Wells, F. L. The relation of practice to individual differences. *Amer. J. Psych.*, 23: Jan., 1912, 75–88.

Whipple, G. M. *Classes for Gifted Children.* Bloomington, Ill., 1919.

Whipple, G. M. Experiments in the education of gifted children. *J. Mich. Schoolmaster's Club*, 1919, pp. 8–23.

Whipple, G. M. The problem of selecting and training gifted children in the public schools. *Bull. Extension Div. Indiana Univ.*, Vol. 4, No. 4, Dec., 1918, pp. 6–16.

Whipple, G. M. The supernormal child. *J. Educ. Psych.*, 2:1911, 164, 287.

Whipple, G. M. Supernormal children, in *Cyclop. of Educ.*, 1913.

Whitney, F. P. Equality and the schools. *Educ.* 33: October, 1912, 84–90.

Whittier State School, Whittier, Cal. *Dept. of Research Bull., No. 6*, Exceptional children in the schools of Santa Ana, Cal., pp. 24–25.

Williams, J. H. Delinquent boys of superior intelligence. *J. of Delinquency*, 1: March, 1916, 33–52.

Williams, T. A. Intellectual precocity. Comparison between John Stuart Mill and the son of Dr. Boris Sidis. *Ped. Sem.*, 18:1911, 85–103.

Witmer, L. Retardation through neglect in children of the rich. Psych. Clinic, 1: 1900, 157–174.

Witmer, L. The training of very bright children. *Psych. Clinic*, 13: Dec., 1919, 88–96.

Witte, K. *The Education of Karl Witte.* (Eng. trans. by L. Wiener, edited by H. A.) Bruce) New York, 1914.

Woburn, Mass. School Committee, Annual Reports, 1903, 1914.

Woodrow, H. *Brightness and Dullness in Children*, Philadelphia, 1919, especially Chs. XIII and XIV.

Woods, Elizabeth L. Provision for the gifted child. *Educ. Adm. and Superv.*, 3:1917, 139–149.

Woolfolk, A. The case of him that hath ten talents. *Virginia J. of Educ.*, 11: September, 1917, 18–22.

Worcester, Mass. School Committee, Annual Reports, 1902, 1904, 1912.

Yoder, A. H. Exceptional children. *Survey*, 7: January, 1912, 1598–1600.

Yoder, A. H. The study of the boyhood of great men. *Ped. Sem.*, 3: 1894, 134–156.

Zauck, C. Sonderklassen f. hevorragend begabte Schüler. *Pädagogische Zeitung*, 41, Feb. 15, 1912, 109–112 (See also 112–114).

VITA

Theodore Spafford Henry was born May 9, 1878, at West Jersey, Stark County, Illinois. He obtained his elementary education in the rural school, and prepared for college in the Academy of Hedding College, Abingdon, Illinois. He received the degree of A.B. from Hedding College in 1903. He was a graduate student in education at the University of Illinois during the summer sessions of 1913, 1914, 1915, and 1916, and the regular school years of 1915–1916 and 1916-1917; and received the degree of A.M. in education in 1916. Throughout the year 1916-1917 he was engaged in a study of gifted children conducted by Professor Guy M. Whipple, under a subsidy from the General Education Board.

His first year of teaching (1903–1904) was in a country school in Warren County, Illinois. From 1904 to 1907, he was in charge of village graded schools at Altona, Illinois (two years), and Melvin, Illinois (one year). From 1907 to 1912 he was superintendent of schools at Elmwood, Illinois, and from 1912 to 1916 at Havana, Illinois. He was instructor in psychology at the Michigan State Normal College, Ypsilanti, Michigan, during the summer session of 1917. Since September 1, 1917, he has been professor of psychology in the Western State Normal School, Kalamazoo, Michigan.

He is a member of Kappa Delta Pi, Phi Delta Kappa, and Sigma Xi. He has published:

A comparison of two recent contributions to the theory of education. *School and Home Education*, September, 1916.

Standards of "good form" in classroom teaching. *School and Home Education*, November, 1916.

The problem method in teaching. *School and Home Education*, February, 1917.

The education and control of the emotions. *Journal of Educational Psychology*, September, 1917.

www.ingramcontent.com/pod-product-compliance
Lightning Source LLC
LaVergne TN
LVHW021419110826

845150LV00007B/1988

* 9 7 8 1 4 2 5 5 7 2 1 2 9 *